PARENT POWER

PARENT POWER

90 Winning Ways to Be Involved and Help Your Child Get the Most Out of School

BY ROBERTA KIRSHBAUM
WITH ROBIN DELLABOUGH

A Seth Godin Production

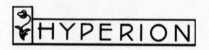

New York

Designed by Wendy Wax

FIRST EDITION
10 9 8 7 6 5 4 3 2 1

Library of Congress Cataloging-in-Publication Data
Kirshbaum, Roberta
     Parent power: 90 winning ways to be involved and help your child get the most out of school / by Roberta Kirshbaum with Robin Dellabough. — 1st ed.
     p.   cm.
     Includes bibliographical references and index.
     ISBN: 0 7868 8329 4
     1. Education—Parent Participation—United States. 2. Teacher-student relationships—United States. I. Dellabough, Robin. II. Title.
LB1048.5.K57 1998
371.19'2—dc21

98–22591
CIP

ACKNOWLEDGMENTS

This book was inspired by the many parents and supportive colleagues whom I have worked with over my years in education. All along the way I have been learning and growing from my experiences with dedicated and inspired leaders and hardworking parents who thought beyond what would benefit only their children. I found out the depths to which caring and commitment could extend from the parents of P.S. 75. I couldn't begin to name them all, but they were true partners in a new endeavor as we envisioned what the school could be and turned it around—together.

My loving friends and relatives have been most supportive, by providing the unfailing enthusiasm and confidence that nourishes inspiration. Becoming a parent myself was the most consciousness-raising experience of my career as an educator. I owe a big debt of gratitude to my children, Alex and Jesse, from whom I learned firsthand how powerful the school experience can be for a child if the parents truly team up with the teachers.

I'd like to thank Robin Dellabough, Sarah Silbert, Ann Weinerman, and everyone at Seth Godin Productions for initiating and supporting the writing of this book, which represents the fruition of a long-standing dream.

Finally and most importantly, I want to thank my husband and friend, Ken, for his support during times when the work is all-consuming. This book would not exist without his valuable insights. The satisfaction I feel from my job would be empty without his love, advice, and support.

CONTENTS

INTRODUCTION

There are parents who think they don't have a place in their child's school. But they do have a place, an important place! Parents should be as comfortable in their kid's classroom as they are in their own living room. But even parents with enormous initiative and creativity often don't know how to reach inside the school. They need a call to loving arms. That's why I'm writing this book.

Think of it as a blueprint for how and why you should take charge of your child's education. *Parent Power* is about how to form your own partnership with each teacher and each administrator your child encounters. Empowering parents to have an ongoing relationship with school personnel is the key to unlocking doors of educational opportunity. And it doesn't have to mean bake sales, boring meetings, or buying gift wrap.

What we really need is a partnership with ongoing support. I've been an educator for twenty-seven years, starting as a teacher. But it was as the principal of P.S. 75 on New York City's Upper West Side that I was able to start applying a secret I had learned as a teacher: Parents care about their child most of all, so throw away the idea of abstract reform and bring in parent power. There's nobody as passionate about a child as his parents. But a "lacy curtain" between parents and teachers still often prevents them from becoming full partners. Parents should feel fully entitled to be in the school, to pick up the phone, and to ask for and receive appropriate help. The ideal partnership is parents and teachers in direct communication, sitting down and setting goals together with a shared vision.

I hope this book will help you establish such a pattern of involvement from the moment your child enters kindergarten. With twenty or thirty parents to one teacher, there's a tremendous pool of potential energy. You can come into the classroom, share your backgrounds, and lend your skills to the school. Programs that augment the curriculum can be developed and run by parents during the school day. That same pool of parents can be tapped as either the foot power or the idea power in bringing resources to the schools. Once we are able to harness that power, there's no end to what can be accomplished. I know this firsthand. I watched it happen at my school. Here is my story:

I first taught at a school in East Harlem and then one in Brooklyn. I loved teaching. My attitude toward principals was that it's a dirty job, but somebody's got to do it. But as time went on, I began to realize that it was the principal who really set the tone of the school. I could only attain a certain level of influence as a teacher, and I wanted to be able to have an impact on more than one class at a time. I wanted to energize a whole school. I gradually became more and more involved in the administrative side of education, from organizing a pilot reading program to serving as an acting principal. I went for a second master's degree in administration, which took two summers and the year in between, and finally, I got my principal's license. I was in no hurry. Before I was really ready to start seriously interviewing, I heard about an opening; I decided to apply for it as a sort of practice exercise.

I knew that P.S. 75 was a K–6 school on West End Avenue in Manhattan. I also knew it had quite a troubled history. Its sterling reputation had tarnished within the previous decade. Student achievement had fallen behind, population had dwindled, and there was a lot of tension and dissension among the principal, staff, and parents. Yet at its core was the essence of what I believed in: a very active parent group and a heterogeneous group of kids. I walked into the interview feeling I had nothing to lose. At a table sat almost twenty parents, a superintendent, and a few teachers. I felt an immediate connection because I was talking with my peers about my favorite subject: education. They were people my age, with children my children's ages.

I told them I had a strong vision. I believed in parent involvement. I believed in working together. I believed in building up a school. And because I had never actually done the job, I was naive enough to believe it could be done. I thought you just had to forge ahead. I think what really convinced them that I was the principal for their school was my answer to the question, "What accomplishment are you proudest of in your career?" I replied, "I can't think of anything I have accomplished by myself. Everything I've done has been as part of a team."

When I started as principal in December 1989, P.S. 75 was an ugly place. The first week I was there, the Inspector General called twice. People called anonymously to report rumors about teachers, or illegal activities like selling black-market skin-care products out of an office. There was tremendous backstabbing and infighting. My charge was to build up the school and bring back the community from private school choices, particularly the middle-class families. When I took over, about seventy-eight percent of the students had a financial status that qualified them for free lunch. By the time I left it was fifty percent free-lunch kids. At first parents were skeptical. They'd ask, "Why should I take a chance and send my child to a school that isn't proven?" And I would say, "Because here you can have input."

It wasn't a question of joining a PTA. I was constantly asking parents, what do you want to do? My philosophy was if you have an idea, we'll make it happen. I held monthly meetings with parents. No grumbling was allowed. If a parent had a complaint, I wanted to hear a solution. And if it was a good solution, I promised to help them work with the teachers. It was like an educational think tank, and once things got started, more and more ideas bubbled up. Some of them were specific to the needs of P.S. 75, but many could work in any school.

I was always careful to consider individual personalities when a program or idea was introduced. I made an effort to really get to know my teachers one-on-one so that I could be as supportive and nurturing as possible. I'd try to match teachers and parents who were compatible. Say one teacher was really uncomfortable with the idea of a parent working in her classroom. Then I'd suggest a parent help her by bringing her students to the library instead. The point is in any educational setting, everyone needs to be sensitive to each other. You don't want teachers feeling bullied by parents or vice versa.

That was exactly what everyone feared with one of our first big efforts. We had been tapped to be a flagship school for a program Nynex was funding. Every teacher would get a phone with a voice-mailbox in their classroom on which they would leave a message for parents to listen to each night, and where parents could leave messages for the teacher. I admit that even I was hesitant to introduce this system. What if parents abused the opportunity and made a lot of trivial nuisance calls? What if teachers left messages about how "bad" the kids were that day? Actually, that did happen and I got a lot of angry complaints from parents the next day!

I quickly realized the key would be to lay out the ground rules in advance. I warned teachers that if they didn't leave a message, their voice-mail would be taken away. I explained that the type of message I wanted was not *The kids were bad today,* but *We had a difficult day and had to regroup.* Or *Today we learned about such and such. We read the story of* Madeline. *Ask your son or daughter to explain why Madeline needed to go to the hospital. Tonight I've assigned the children pages 5 and 6 in their spelling books. If you heard this message, have your child come in and tell me the secret password: monkey.*

Next I had to tell parents not to leave messages such as *I'm picking my child up early today* or *How could you have done this to my child?* Not once in the seven years we had the voice-mail system did a parent abuse it. Instead, it turned out to be a wonderful tool. Parents were respectful and really appreciated the chance to find out more about their child's day, what he was learning, and his homework assignments. It made them feel much more connected to the school, especially for those who worked during the day. Others were grateful for the system because they still felt uncomfortable in the presence of teachers, as if they were suddenly back in school themselves. It was less threatening to call and listen to a teacher on the phone.

I think this is one of the best ideas for increasing parent involvement, and it can be modified depending on the school. Nowadays, for instance, a lot of schools use e-mail or post what's going on every day on a Web page. There's a computer program that sets up voice messaging as well.

At P.S. 75 parents developed a Reading Garden, a pleasant outdoor space where children can go in good weather to read quietly. Authors' Day was a celebration of books written and bound by students. We held a formal ceremony, complete with invitations to parents, a breakfast, a master of ceremonies, and a public reading of each book.

"Storytelling Is a Family Affair" was one of my favorite projects. We hooked up with the Confabulator Program, conceived of and administered by the Cornell University

Cooperative Extension Service. (Confabulator is a Middle Ages term describing those who tell stories "in which souls take delight.") Parents could attend a six-hour-a-week course given by Cornell if they wished. Then they were invited into classrooms once a week to tell their stories. One parent from Zaire described his adventure with a poisonous snake. A mother told of her childhood in Ireland; a father shared a story about his great-great-grandfather's mail-order false teeth. He then unveiled a quilt made by his daughter's great-great-great-grandmother and told another story about sewing.

All the parents were celebrated this way, not just those with interesting jobs or skills. No wonder the children loved these sessions. Their souls really did take delight in hearing such a colorful tapestry of tales.

"Learning by Baking" was a unit my first grade teachers came up with after attending a two-week curriculum-writing course at Bank Street College. The kids took field trips to bakeries, bagel shops, and pizzerias where parents or friends worked. At a bialy bakery they learned about the roll named after the town of Bialystok in Eastern Europe, and they visited a Dominican bakery. They conducted yeast experiments, learned to count by putting raisins in bread slices, read stories about baking bread, grew wheat and corn, ground grain into flour, and invited parents to share family bread recipes and to bake bread in the classroom.

Other ideas were in direct response to a lack in the school, as opposed to supplementing what was already in place. When we started losing teacher's aides due to budget cuts, a parent volunteered to organize a group of other parents to tutor children on a regular basis. Music had been axed back in 1974. So I was thrilled when a professor in the music department at Montclair State College—who wanted his daughter to attend P.S. 75—offered to have his graduate students come and initiate a band program. In exchange he gave his students college credits.

We also found tremendous support by reaching out to community organizations. We were especially fortunate to be in a city like New York with its incredible cultural resources, but it took parents to take advantage of them. And they did. From bringing in dance troupes to taking kids to Carnegie Hall, from the Teachers College to the Child Welfare Association, parents constantly reached further into the community rather than relying only on us. The Jewish Community Center, for example, paid for a reading specialist to train and supervise older students from other schools, as well as senior citizens, as tutors. Once trained, these tutors helped our first graders learn to read. The Manhattan Chess Club sent us a member to teach chess and to organize a club.

Some of the things parents did were really simple and concrete. They cleaned rugs and washed windows. One father went to the library each week with a wagon and checked out forty books. The teacher then made sure those books weren't lost, so, as always, it was a partnership.

Parents got involved in some down-to-earth problem solving. We had a lice problem we simply could not get rid of. I know I'm not the expert on everything, so I asked the parents for help. We had meetings about the lice, discussed whether or not we had to remove the rugs, and any other measures we could take. Working together, we finally did conquer the lice.

Another parent worked in advertising. She noticed we had painted all the dingy, dilapidated outside doors, but inside remained untouched. We weren't allowed to paint on the walls, but she found some well-known illustrators and artists to paint murals on all the inside doors. They worked with the students to tie the murals to lessons they were learning at the time. All the doors are now painted in different, gorgeous, bright designs. How could I have said no to that idea? The worst thing that could have happened was that we'd have to paint it over.

The results of parent power were astounding. Academic scores began to rise dramatically. Teachers, who had been badly demoralized, were now an eager, enthusiastic team. The school was transformed from broken down to a cheerful, safe environment. A once-bare-bones library became rich in books. An after-school program offered sports, music, science, and ceramics. There were at least three students applying for every opening each September and a long waiting list. For two years in a row, P.S. 75 was chosen as one of the best elementary schools in New York State in a national magazine contest. We were nominated by our local U.S. congressman.

More significant were the halls and classrooms filled with smiling, shining faces of alert, engaged, and happy students. The staring-into-space syndrome—too prevalent in the past — was gone, and the once-empty seats were filled to capacity.

Instead of fights during recess, I witnessed lots of healthy, cooperative play.

I believe we in education should constantly reinvent ourselves, otherwise, we're not learning anything. By 1996 I felt I had brought all I could to P.S. 75. The school was thriving. Everything was in place for someone else to take over. Much as I enjoyed the excitement of an urban setting and the individuals I had come to love, I was ready to move on to new challenges. I wanted to stir up my creative juices. So when I was offered the principal's job for a school in the suburbs, I took it. It's been an enormous and fascinating change.

In this district, parents were not regularly invited to work in classrooms. I was surprised to find they didn't have an Open School Week. So there wasn't a strong pattern of parental involvement in the classrooms. There was an active PTA that raised funds and provided a lot of financial support for programs. Yet even in this relatively well-off school there was plenty of need for parental energy and enthusiasm. I knew the first step was to make parents feel more welcome inside the school. Although they were included in specially planned events, and they ran a book fair and helped in the library, I wanted them even more involved. The more parents are in the classroom, the more they become part of an ongoing partnership based on trust.

But I also had to go slowly. Every system has its own "culture," defined as "because that's the way we do things." I couldn't change this school culture too quickly. So we invited parents in to see their children working with computers. The parents loved it and in general it was a great success. There were some kindergartners who had trouble when their parents arrived, when they left, or if they couldn't come. There were complaints and criticisms. But I felt this was a small price to pay.

As our society has changed, we've lost a certain connection, a sense of community. The school is one stable place where people should come together. Now schools provide after-school programs. We have night events, we have whole-family workshops. Families get together around school events, the school life. It's almost taking the place of what churches did. But PTA meetings for working parents are hard. If you work, then you don't want to leave your child at night, too. It's sometimes much better to have an event on a Saturday morning, a family workshop where parents are working alongside their children.

Once we held a family conference where people signed up and we had box lunches. At my present school, the music teacher planned a study-piano-at-home program and did a forty-five-minute workshop creating music with the parents and kids. Our computer teacher talked about how parents could work with their children and then families made family crests on the computers. A dancer did an arts-in-education workshop for parents and children together. The art teacher did a calligraphy class, and a puppet-making workshop was offered where parents and children played and had fun in an educational context.

This family workshop approach has been consistently

effective in bringing parents into the process of children's learning. Other educators often want to know why this approach works well. So I've put a lot of thought into the reasons:

- It doesn't isolate the constituent groups.
- It maximizes quality time that is so precious for all of today's parents.
- It affords parents a chance to peek into the life of their children as learners, within the school context.
- It lets parents get to know teachers in a nonthreatening way.

On a more informal basis, I've encouraged parents to let me know if they hear of anything or have any connections they think might benefit the school or the children. As a result a parent let us know about an exhibit at the Museum of Modern Art featuring a Philip Johnson glass house. He told us how to arrange a class trip there. My wish list for my current school includes creating a greenhouse and an astronomy lab. I fully expect that it will be parents who grant my wish. There are also many talented people in the community who aren't employed outside the home. I'm slowly contacting them and asking them to come share their talents. This revitalizes the idea that parent involvement means more than helping kids do their homework, or even joining the PTA.

There's an anonymous quote I stumbled across years ago that really sums up how I feel about an educator's life and a life in education. I've had it hanging in all my offices and it hangs on my office wall today:

> *Coming together is a beginning;*
> *Keeping together is progress;*
> *Working together is success.*

Author's Note: I've made a few editorial decisions in order to make things as clear and simple as possible. I've alternated between *he* and *she* when referring to children. Parents' organizations call themselves PTSA, PTO, and PTA. For the sake of consistency, I've used PTA throughout the book.

Instead of cramming the main text of the book with lots of educational terms, I include a separate glossary of the more technical words a parent might hear during a child's school years. These words are not necessarily mentioned in the ninety winning ways, but I think you'll find reading the definitions useful.

CHAPTER ONE

CLASS ACTION

A parent is a child's first teacher. It's in the warm, safe, friendly home environment that children learn how to learn. Studies have shown that the more children feel at home in school, the more they learn. So it makes sense that if they feel teachers and parents are working together and school is an extension of home, they feel more connected to their schools and are more successful students. This fairly recent knowledge is a new wrinkle in the face of school reform; the result is a national push to have parents involved in their child's education.

But wait a minute. Aren't parents naturally interested in their child? Why do we need any special effort to get parents more involved?

It happens so imperceptibly, a parent may not realize what's happening for years. A child begins kindergarten. There is daily contact with the teacher. Impromptu conversations take place as the parent shuttles the child back and forth. Regularly scheduled conferences occur at least twice a year. The parent is encouraged to spend time in the classroom, observing, or even participating in cooking projects or short expeditions. Enthusiasm and interest run high as the parent eagerly asks about the child's day and shares in the wonderment of learning. The parent tries to make time for school events, evening meetings, no doubt joins the PTA and volunteers for at least one or two activities. And the child welcomes the parent's involvement, basks in the shared experience even as she is slowly, slowly growing up and away.

Eventually—usually by middle school—parents are no longer welcome in the child's world. Even the best-intentioned parent can wake up with a barely recognizable child, a young person who goes to a school that is so unfamiliar to the parent, it might as well be another planet. A parent has to struggle to discover the tiniest bit of information about an adolescent's day. It's difficult to reach high school teachers, conferences are rare, and there's little opportunity or time to volunteer. It's all too easy to simply let a child drift off in an educational haze—and not even be aware of what's happening.

Unfortunately, as parents struggle to keep up with their own demanding, hectic schedules, fewer and fewer of them feel they have enough time for their families at all, let alone to get involved in their child's education. Only thirty-one percent of employed parents meet frequently with their child's teacher to discuss school progress. Only fifty-two percent of employed parents regularly attend school activities. Only thirty-six percent of employed parents even help their child with homework.

Such benign neglect is a costly mistake, however. The consequences for children are dramatic: Academic achievement plummets as this parental involvement decreases, as measured objectively by SAT scores, National Assessment of Education Progress, and international comparisons. Between budget cuts, higher salaries, and dropping test scores, it's little wonder the American educational system is in trouble. But even more troubling to me is the change in society: increased drug abuse, teenage pregnancy, violence, and a general sense of malaise or disengagement among many kids.

For thirty years, we've had research clearly showing a link between parental involvement and educational achievement—and that holds true regardless of socioeconomic levels. In one study of fourth grade reading comprehension, students with highly involved parents scored *forty-four* points ahead of their peers whose parents were less involved. Students whose parents remain active in the PTA consistently perform above average.

Parental Involvement Is a Necessity

Many studies and surveys have concluded that the more involved a parent stays with a child's education, the better that child will do both academically and emotionally.

The U.S. Department of Education found the evidence for parental involvement leading to student success so strong that it launched a comprehensive campaign in 1994. Called "Partnership for Family Involvement in Education," its mission is to "increase opportunities for families to be more involved in their children's learning at school and at home and to use family-school-community partnerships to strengthen schools and improve student achievement." More than 3,000 family, school, community, employer, and religious groups have already joined the grassroots movement. They encourage everything from better home-school communication to providing leave time to attend parent conferences and volunteer in school. They provide parent training and child care, organize before- and after-school activities, help make streets safer for children, and sponsor cultural programs. U.S. Secretary of Education Richard W. Riley sums up the Partnership with this motto: "Better Education Is Everybody's Business."

Temple University professor Laurence Steinberg led a team of researchers who surveyed 20,000 teenagers and their parents. The Steinberg study discovered that "being an involved parent actually leads to student success. If we saw two students with equal grades in school at one time and followed them over the course of the next year, we would find that the student whose parents were more involved in his or her education would earn better grades over time than the student whose parents were less involved." This sounds like a compelling enough reason for a parent to become involved, wouldn't you think? Yet the same study found that more than half the students said they could bring home grades of C or worse without their parents getting upset; nearly one-third of students said their parents have no idea how they are doing in school; and only about one-fifth of parents consistently attend school programs, while more than forty percent never do.

According to a study of 17,000 students by the National

Center for Education Statistics, in two-parent households where both were highly involved, fifty-one percent of the children got mostly **A**s; only twenty-seven percent, or almost *half* that number, received mostly **A**s if neither parent was very involved. Education Commissioner Pascal Forgione Jr. was quoted as saying the study shows "that if involvement by both parents is low, a child's chance of success is dramatically reduced."

Now I can imagine those of you who have teenagers protesting that your children don't want you to be involved. You're just trying to keep peace with them. But are you absolutely sure that what your adolescent *says* he wants and what he *really* wants are the same thing? In a survey by the National Commission on Children, almost half of older teenagers said they *would* like their parents to be involved in their education. As a parent myself, I know this is true. I've tried to work with my two teenaged sons' teachers as a partner in their education. If there's a problem, I try to meet with the teacher before it gets out of hand. When my son Alex was having some trouble in an advanced math class, I went to the teacher. She told me Alex was very able, but he didn't have a lot of confidence. I asked whether we should get a tutor, and she said no, but to have him come in early. We made a plan to stay in touch with each other. She was very open to doing that, and instead of a disaster, it was a successful year for Alex.

I like to say PTA should also stand for Parents Take Action. I want you to start believing that you can be a consumer advocate for your child from the beginning and that you need to continue lobbying throughout the school years. It's worth every effort you can possibly make.

How It Can Work

Parents can reach out in many different ways, as a group and as individuals. In fact, it's safe to say there isn't a school district in this country that can't use parents as partners. And I don't mean just for frills or extras. Most districts have cut their budgets to the leanest levels as teachers' salaries have risen and voters have protested paying higher school taxes. Art, music, languages, gifted programs, physical education—these are usually the first to go. I know one small high school in a relatively affluent community, for example, that prided itself on its Latin curriculum. When the budget simply couldn't pay for teaching Latin anymore, a local education foundation stepped in to save it. (See page 162 for information on starting this kind of foundation.)

In the nationwide Home Instruction Program for Preschool Youngsters (HIPPY), a paraprofessional meets with parents of four- and five-year-olds to help them prepare their children for school. The program is designed to increase parents' self-esteem and to improve their children's cognitive abilities. The program also enables parents to meet for group discussions. This program is now available in twenty-six states, and teachers have rated HIPPY graduates as better adapted to the classroom and more likely to do well in school.

An oral tradition program in a school with a very diverse

population is another avenue for involving parents. Parents who don't feel comfortable with English might not ordinarily feel comfortable speaking in the classroom. But when families are invited to tell their stories and share something of their heritage, the children get very involved. The class learns to ask and answer questions. All the children feel a sense of pride because their parents can contribute equally. The teacher is exposed to the children's background, improving communication. This creates a sense of family in a classroom that is impossible to generate without parental involvement.

What is school for? The point of school is to help children become joyful, lifelong learners through reading and discovery, so they become the most they can be. The teacher is coach, providing information, but mostly motivating a child to go to the nth degree. We have to create programs that enable children to become self-starters. Not every teacher can do that; that is why we need parents.

What Parental Involvement Does for Your Child

Think of school as a puzzle. Parents and teachers possess different pieces of the puzzle. One piece is that kids do better when they know that their parents care about their school. Kids feel proud when they know their parents have contributed. It makes them feel more connected. It's important to point it out and not leave them to draw their own conclusions. That's why I give parent volunteers ribbons that say, "I'm a very important parent" and tell them "You must wear it. You must have your child ask you why you're wearing that corny ribbon. You must say, 'Because I was honored by the school today for what I did.'" It's important. It's not given to every parent. I could give them a little pin that the kids wouldn't notice. But I really want the child to ask about it and to give the parent a chance to share.

We know there isn't one average child—every child has a million strengths. We don't teach to the collective middle anymore. The more opportunities and resources there are, the more we have a chance to make a difference in a child's life, to affect the rest of his life. The more ideas parents bring in the better. They percolate. The more areas we can touch on in school, whether it's baking, botany, or blowing glass, the more children we might reach.

Throughout this book, whenever I use the word "parent," please understand I really mean both mom and dad, if there are two parents; grandmother or grandfather, if that's who is raising a child; or whomever else is a legal guardian. The days are long past when only a mother is expected to show up at a parent-teacher conference or to be a class parent. A father's involvement is equally important.

For instance, a volunteer effort involving fathers I particularly applaud is the Security Dads in Beech Grove City, Indiana. Fathers in the schools there provide a visible male parental presence at school-sponsored sporting events, dances, skating parties, and other student-based activities. The Security Dads ensure proper behavior, evict troublemakers when necessary, and generally keep the peace. Fathers are recruited through requests made at parent meetings, student referrals, and home visits. The result? Paternal involvement in school and children's activities has increased and students behave much better at all these events.

It *is* possible for a parent to have a really bad idea. One of my favorite examples is the parent who wanted to bring a dead animal into the classroom to share with students. Most ideas are terrific, though. It's usually more a matter of bad timing than a bad idea. In the following pages, I try to steer you in the right direction to avoid efforts backfiring, to help you avoid stepping on school personnel toes, to get everybody working together in partnership and with trust.

There are three important pieces of advice I can offer you before you dip into the rest of the book. One is that making a commitment to being an involved parent is crucial. It's like marriage. We know that a huge percentage of marriages end in divorce, and I think it's often because there is a lack of commitment. If you tell a teacher you will come in to help with math, it's best to commit to every Monday morning at nine, and then show up consistently.

Second, please, please read these suggestions as ways to help *all* the children. If you focus only on what your own child is going to get out of whatever you do, you're shortchanging everyone. Keep in mind that the other kids you help today inhabit your child's world and will someday be the adults who make up our society. A society is only as good as its citizens.

The third point in becoming a successfully involved parent

is to stay sensitive to the other person, whether it's a teacher, a child, another parent, or a staff person. It's basically the Golden Rule. I urge you to go to your school with the attitude, *I want to form a partnership, which means we have to work together. How can we make this work? What do we have to do?* The teacher or administrator might say, *I can always use the help, but I don't like parents in the classroom. I do need somebody to run off copies of lessons, though.* Rather than giving up or getting mad, you could say, *Okay. I really want to be in a classroom. Is there any way that we can work around that? Might you want me to come in during writing time and not interfere with your teaching?* The point is you need to be able to talk, to get your cards on the table.

The tools are within *everyone's* grasp to make a difference in education and in our families. Once you have these tools, you will be equipped to build a limitless future with your children, and for your children.

CHAPTER TWO

FROM HOME BASE

Twenty-five things you can do, without leaving the comfort of your home, that will have a positive impact on a child's education.

Some of the suggestions in this chapter are very simple, while others take more effort. The point is to pick and choose those that best fit into your life and lifestyle.

1 FIRST THINGS FIRST.

One of the most obvious, yet neglected, areas of parental involvement is making sure your child starts out each school day from as strong a position as possible. This means she's had enough rest, eaten a good breakfast, is wearing comfortable clothes for the weather, and has had enough time to get ready without too much rushing.

2 INVITE YOUR CHILD'S TEACHER HOME.

Whether it's for tea, brunch, dinner, or dessert, nothing telegraphs your respect for their importance in your child's life than such a warm welcome. Nothing makes your own child feel more important than entertaining a teacher at home. It's the perfect way to make the partnership more personal. Of course, you will want to be sensitive to the teacher's time constraints. If he's a young single teacher, he might welcome a nice dinner. If she's a working mother, she'd probably rather fit any socializing into the school day. Pick up your cues from the teacher, and stay flexible with your invitation.

3 CLIP AND SEND ARTICLES OF POSSIBLE INTEREST TO YOUR CHILD'S SCHOOL.

This is a gentle way to encourage enrichment activities in the classroom as well as to get the teacher to think of you as an individual. For example, during the presidential election, you notice a newspaper is offering a student debate series for free to teachers. Or you edit a newsletter on gender equity, so you send a copy to school, knowing the principal is looking for ways to retain female students' interest in math.

You can send material in via your child; or by dropping it in the teacher's mailbox, usually located in the school's main office; or by mailing through the post office. Whatever system you choose, attach a short note that makes it clear you're sending it purely in case it happens to be of use or interest. You don't want to seem as if you're putting any pressure whatsoever on a teacher to do anything more than look at the article. On the other hand, from my experience, it's just this kind of tiny effort that often turns into a great educational opportunity for the children.

4 READ WITH YOUR CHILD.

Reading is the single most important predictor of, factor in, and influence on your child's school success. If you do nothing else suggested in this entire book, do read as often as possible together, and in front of, your child. You can't start the habit too soon or keep it up too long.

Here are a few suggestions you can act on right now:

- Have plenty of reading material around the house, including newspapers, magazines, and library books.

- Read aloud together every day. If bedtime doesn't work for your family, try at breakfast. But do try.

- Play family board games, such as Scrabble, Boggle, or Dictionary, to help build vocabulary.

- Memorize poems to recite together on car trips or waiting in lines.

- Have family letter-writing sessions. Encourage your child to write to grandma or have a regular pen pal.

- Start an exciting book with many chapters. Each day end at a particularly dramatic point so that your child can't wait to hear what happens next.

- Don't worry too much about what your child is reading, as long as she's reading. The goal is to establish a lifelong habit; the content can change over time.

- Be sure there is a place with good light and comfortable seating where your child can read at any time.

- Give your child books or gift certificates to bookstores and encourage other relatives to do the same. I know one woman who always gives her six nieces and nephews a book for birthdays and at Christmas. She's now known as the "book aunt." She was inspired by her brother-in-law

who started the tradition when her
own children were little.

No matter what age your child, keep
reading together!

Books on Reading

There are some excellent books devoted to the subject of children and reading. For more specific help on
how to foster a love of reading in your child, I recommend the following titles:

*For Reading Out Loud: A Guide to Sharing Books
with Children,* by Margaret Mary Kimmel
and Elizabeth Segel.

The Read-Aloud Handbook, by Jim Trelease.

*The New York Times Parent's Guide to the Best
Books for Children,* by Eden Lipson.

Reading for the Love of It, by Michele Landsberg.

The RIF Guide to Encouraging Young Readers,
by Ruth Graves.

Timeless Classics (pamphlet that lists 400 books
published since 1960, appropriate for ages/
grades K–12), Consumer Information Center
(719) 948-3334.

The Uses of Enchantment, by Bruno Bettelheim.

5 ASK ABOUT YOUR CHILD'S DAY.

Ask in the most effective way possible. Don't blurt out, *How was school today?* the first minute you see your child. Such a point-blank question will make your child respond as if you've taken aim at her. Instead, try the following techniques:

- Don't ask anything at all—at least not right away. Give your child a chance to unwind, have a snack, put away her things. Chances are that she'll be in a much more receptive mood for conversation after she's made the transition from school to home.

- Try to start a conversation, rather than an inquisition. Tell your child something about your day. Sometimes describing an embarrassing or funny situation is all it takes to have your offspring pour out a similar story.

- Be as specific as possible. Instead of *How was social studies?* try asking *Did Ms. Dolan start that unit on the Middle East you were looking forward to yet?* or *How did you feel about your oral presentation in science?*

- Ask *What did you learn?* instead of *What did you get?* Taking the emphasis off the numbers not only sends a message about the importance of learning over grades, but it gives your child a chance to show off what he knows.

- Turn your after-school chat into a ritual by asking, *What was the best part of your day?* and *What was the worst part?*

Conversation Starters

Dr. Linda Albert of the National PTA has additional suggestions for getting your kids to talk about what they're doing in ways that will be fun for everyone:

- The Family Merry-Go-Round: Make an I-statement each member of the family has to complete, like "One of the things I did well today was ..." or "The most surprising thing I learned today was ..." This game makes it fun for your kids to talk about their day.

- Table Talk: Talk about what your kids are learning over the dinner table. Pass around papers and tests for discussion and admiration.

- Classroom Chronicles: Make a tradition of having your children chronicle their days on cassette tape as soon as they get home from school. Later, listen to it together as a way of sparking conversation about what they've learned and done.

6 LISTEN CAREFULLY TO YOUR CHILD.

Listen to both her words and her nonverbal cues to get a better idea of how things are going educationally. Does she come bursting in the door, bright-eyed and upbeat? Or does she drag herself home and seem tired all the time? Has she developed a nervous tic since she started studying algebra? Or does she seem to be exuding more self-confidence than ever? Children don't always know what's causing them to feel a certain way, or even how they're feeling. If they do know, they might not be able to express it verbally. It's up to a connected, involved parent to be an emotional detective.

7 MAKE A FAMILY CALENDAR.

Be sure to mark school events on it. Use the calendar the school district sends to every resident so you don't miss out on special times. This is especially important if your child has a tendency—and what child does not?—to lose notices about meetings, conferences, trips, dances, and so on. I know of at least one classroom visiting day when only one parent showed up: She had marked the day parents were invited to visit their children's classrooms on the family calendar. Of course, the family calendar works best if you then try to attend as many extracurricular events as possible.

8 DESIGN A SCHOOL CHECKLIST.

Are you unsure of how to get involved? It might seem overwhelming because you don't really know where to start or if your school could even use any improvement. In my experience, there is no such thing as a perfect school. Any school in the world can be improved in some way. You'll be better able to pinpoint where your help is most needed if you take an inventory of your school's strengths and weaknesses. (There's a sample checklist you can adapt for your school on pages 34–35.)

Of course, this is only the first step. Once you've completed a checklist, be sure to share it with as many other parents, teachers, school board members, and administrators as possible. Then, together, you can try to come up with concrete plans with some sense of what's most important or pressing.

Sample School Checklist

	GOOD	PROBLEM
CURRICULUM		
Has music classes	☐	☐
Has art classes	☐	☐
Has physical education	☐	☐
Has foreign language	☐	☐
Has science instruction	☐	☐
Has computer training	☐	☐
Has special reading teachers	☐	☐
Has special math teachers	☐	☐
Has gifted and talented program	☐	☐
TEACHERS AND OTHER STAFF		
Has adequate number of certified staff	☐	☐
Has unfilled positions	☐	☐
Has an average class size	☐	☐
Has sufficient nurse coverage	☐	☐
Has a school psychologist	☐	☐
Has a librarian	☐	☐
Has enough substitute teachers on call	☐	☐
BOOKS AND OTHER RESOURCES		
Has enough textbooks	☐	☐
Has textbooks in good condition and up to date	☐	☐
Has a well-stocked library	☐	☐
Has adequate VCRs, photocopiers, etc.	☐	☐
Has computers and appropriate software	☐	☐

	GOOD	PROBLEM
PHYSICAL ENVIRONMENT		
Has a roof in good condition	❐	❐
Has been checked for asbestos, radon, lead, and other toxic materials	❐	❐
Has working windows in good repair	❐	❐
Has floors and walls in good condition	❐	❐
Has safe playground areas	❐	❐
Has large enough gym facilities	❐	❐
Has large enough library facilities	❐	❐
Has a clean, safe place for children to eat	❐	❐
Has a good security system	❐	❐
PARENTAL INVOLVEMENT		
Makes parents feel welcome in school	❐	❐
Invites participation in hiring teachers	❐	❐
Has an active parents' organization	❐	❐
Holds regular back-to-school nights	❐	❐
Has frequent parent-teacher conferences	❐	❐
Encourages parents to visit children's classroom	❐	❐
Involves parents in teacher evaluation	❐	❐
Regularly sends home information on activities, curriculum, and other topics	❐	❐

9 HELP WITH HOMEWORK.

This is one of the most direct links between the classroom and the living room. Besides giving teachers a chance to gauge students' understanding of the material taught in class, homework gives parents a chance to see what their child is learning during the day and to take an active role in helping. There are entire books on the subject of helping with homework, and I recommend you read at least one. But meanwhile here are some general tips.

There are several ways to help your child with her homework, and most of them have nothing to do with telling them what two plus two is or how to spell "weird." You can help your child best by maintaining a work-ready environment at home. Try these suggestions:

- Establish a daily routine for your child, including the same period every day set aside for homework. It doesn't matter whether it's right after school, or before or after dinner. The important thing is to make it consistent.

- Keep a monthly chart of homework assignments.

- Create a regular quiet time when the whole family—not just the child—reads or works, giving your child a chance to focus on his homework without feeling deprived or like he's missing out on something.

- Keep one room or area clean, quiet, and well-lit, and set it aside as a work space for your child.

- Allow your child to work in the style that suits him best. Some children work better lying in bed and listening to music, while others need to sit at a desk with no distractions.

When it comes to the homework itself, the amount of help you should give your child varies, depending on his age and study habits. Research has shown that in the elementary grades, homework can be a valuable means of extending your child's learning time and forming good study habits. One of the most important things you can do for your child is to let him know you think homework is important. Make sure your elementary school child understands the directions, and maybe show him how to do a problem. But remember, you don't need to do it for him—a wrong answer is an indicator to the teacher that your child needs more help.

Feel free to speak with the teacher if your child seems to be taking much too long or no time at all with her homework, or if you don't understand your child's work. Teachers usually have a very accurate sense of how much time each homework subject should be taking each child. Plus, any information you can give teachers about what's going on at home with homework helps them meet your child's needs.

10 WRITE A NOTE TO YOUR CHILD'S TEACHER.

Explain any absence, preferably in advance, in writing. This simple act of respect reinforces the idea that you want to keep the teacher in the loop—and vice versa. It establishes a *pattern* of communication. And nothing is worse than inadvertently annoying the teacher by forcing him to rearrange the day's plan at the last minute or to call you at work. (See sample notes to teachers on pages 40–41.)

11 PAY ATTENTION TO TV.

There's no question that TV plays a huge role in children's lives today. As schools struggle to increase reading and SAT scores, and to make programs that excite children about reading, they do little about the most serious threat to reading competency—TV. We need to acknowledge its impact and learn how to use the good and minimize the bad.

The first thing you can do is regulate the TV your kids watch, both in terms of time and content. Try to make sure the programming your children watch:

- Is geared to your child's level of understanding.
- Provides good role models.
- Shows problems being solved in realistic ways.
- Sends the kinds of messages you want your child to hear.
- Has humor appropriate for your child's age level.

Other ways to regulate how your child watches TV include setting limits on the amount of time, or requiring that homework and chores be done first. A more subtle influence is the number of TVs

Sample Notes to a Teacher

Dear Mr. Burns,

Jamie will be absent tomorrow due to a doctor's appointment in the city. I'd appreciate it if you could send him home today with any work he might miss. I hope this isn't too inconvenient. Thank you so much.

Yours truly,
Rita Milo

Dear Ms. Wilson,

Please excuse Christie's absence yesterday due to a family emergency. I hope she will be able to make up any work she might have missed. Thanks very much.

Sincerely,
Jon Berry

Dear Ms. Collins,

Our family will be traveling out of the country for
two weeks this spring. I realize Lisa will need to
make up quite a bit of classwork. Could we get
together to come up with a plan so that she can
get a head start on some work before we leave?
We also think this trip will be a wonderful
learning opportunity for her. Perhaps you
could suggest a concrete assignment relating to
the country we're visiting to help her get even
more out of the experience?

    Please call me at your convenience at either
work (666-5555) or home (666-7777).

Talk to you soon,
Dorothy Nelson

you have, and where they are placed in the house. The fewer TV sets you have in the house, the less available it is to your children. And they'll probably be less likely to plop down in front of the tube if it's all the way down in the basement. You can discourage them from watching TV by encouraging them to do other things. Suggest they take a bike ride, read a book, or play a game. If your child seems reluctant, offer to take part in the activity with her, or propose she call the neighbors and invite them to play along. Encouraging social relationships over TV-watching increases a child's interaction with the real world.

A common mistake parents make is to let the TV be a babysitter for their child. Instead, try to sit and watch it with him. Discuss the content of the shows you watch. Not only does this give you more control over what your child watches but it improves your child's interaction with what he sees—instead of being a passive recipient, he's thinking and talking about what he watches.

You can increase your child's learning from TV by:

- Having him plan ahead for the shows he's going to watch.

- Asking him afterwards about what happened.

- Reinforcing the concepts presented on the show (especially true with educational shows).
- Discussing the nature of TV—the difference between reality and fantasy, what commercials are about and for, how TVs work.

12 DON'T BE AFRAID TO ASK FOR SPECIFIC HELP FOR YOUR CHILD.

From tutoring to extra TLC, you never know how much help you may be able to get from your school if you don't ask. It doesn't have to be a formal request. Sometimes a quiet word with the right teacher, aide, coach, nurse, or secretary is all that's necessary. Start by asking the person if it's a good time to talk. Then briefly describe your child's situation: he's having a hard time with the death of his grandmother, or he's lost in French class, or he's eager to go further in math. Often you don't need to do more than that for the school staff to offer a concrete suggestion: read a book to the whole class on dealing with death, tutor the French student at lunch, or provide enrichment material for the math whiz. If such help is not forthcoming, go ahead and ask the person to do something for or with your child. Be as specific as possible.

Just be careful, though, that you don't ask for the environment to be changed too much to accommodate your child. It is in your child's best interest to learn how to get along in the school as it is. This will prepare him for the "real" world later on.

One fifth grader in Colorado was enrolled in the school's gifted and talented program, which met once a week. His mom noticed that on those days, he came home glowing with excitement about what he'd been doing in that class. Obviously, her son could only benefit from more contact with such an exceptional teacher. She made a point of speaking to the teacher and described how challenged her son was in his class and how very much he seemed to need and thrive on such extra intellectual stimulation. To her delight, the teacher immediately offered to meet with her son and his best friend, another bright student, twice a week over lunch for some brain-teasing. It became one of the best years of her son's schooling.

13 FAMILIARIZE YOURSELF WITH YOUR SCHOOL'S CURRICULUM.

If your school doesn't send home each year an overview of what your child is expected to learn, call and request one. By reading this description, you will get a broad, overarching sense of what your child will be learning and why. It will help put individual units of instruction into a clearer context. You'll know why, for example, your child is studying Homer one semester and Dickens the next. Curricula range from little more than a checklist of topics to a detailed catalogue, as you will see from the examples of kindergarten and fourth grade curricula for a suburban school on pages 226–232 in the Appendix.

14 FIND OUT IF YOUR SCHOOL "TRACKS" CHILDREN ACCORDING TO ABILITY.

Tracking is the century-old practice of grouping students according to academic ability. Advocates say tracking allows teachers to better adjust their style and curriculum to suit each class. A more homogeneous class allows stronger students to move ahead and gives slower students the chance to speak freely without feeling intimidated. Critics of tracking claim it goes against the philosophy of equal-opportunity education. Once a student is placed in a lower track, she may feel discouraged and unmotivated and have trouble improving her academic performance. Critics also object that tracking decisions often are based on standardized tests, and a very small difference in scores can divide students into different tracks.

As a parent, it is important for you to understand your school's tracking program. If the school does track, it might be a rigid track system in which a student is placed in one track for all academic classes. Placement for this kind of tracking is usually based on grade point average, or one test score, which can be unfair or inaccurate, since most individuals are better in some areas than others. Other schools have tracking only for some subjects. In this kind of system, placement is usually based on teacher recommendation or standardized testing in that subject.

Here are some questions you might want to ask your child's teacher or a school guidance counselor:

- Is there tracking in our schools?
- Are students tracked for all classes or only in some subjects?
- How many tracks are there?

- How are the tracking decisions made?

- Do parents have a say about where their child is placed?

- Once my child has been placed in a certain track, how hard is it for her to move up from that track when and if she is ready?

- Are the tracking placements reevaluated on a regular basis?

- Is the curriculum (the textbook and teaching materials) the same for all tracks of a class?

- Do the different tracks have the same teacher? If not, how are teachers assigned different tracks?

If you or your child are uncomfortable with the way your schools handle tracking, or with where your child has been placed, contact the teacher or the guidance department. If they can't resolve your concerns, they may at least be able to provide some helpful information.

15 WRITE A LETTER TO YOUR CHILD'S SCHOOL PRINCIPAL IN THE SPRING.

While you can't ask for a specific teacher, you *can* carefully describe your child's strengths and weak-

IF YOU'RE A
K–1 GRADE PARENT

Volunteer to be an in-class assistant for one hour
a week. **31**
Take your child to the library. **23**
Keep a file for your child's schoolwork. **17**
Share a collection or a custom. **42**
Design a school checklist. **8**

nesses as a student and request the principal make a special effort to place your child with the most appropriate teacher in the next grade. (See sample letters on pages 50–51.) Send your letter before the placement process starts to optimize your chance of getting results. Often schools want to match families with the teacher who will work best with particular children.

A Kansas couple with three children in the third through tenth grades swears by this approach. Each year they've written a letter their kids got the "best" teachers. The one year they neglected to write was the year their eldest got a teacher who was subsequently fired.

16 HANDLE REPORT CARDS EFFECTIVELY.

First, think about where and when you look at your child's report card. It's tempting to rip it open the minute you greet your child at the bus stop or pick her up in the car. But you can't really give it your full, undivided attention at those moments. Make it clear to your child you want to take your time reviewing and calmly discussing her report card with her.

Ask your child, *Is this what you expected? Is there anything that surprises you? How do you feel about this report card?* If there's something she doesn't like, try to talk to her about why she feels that way. Listen to what she has to say. You may be able to help your child set goals or figure out how to avoid being disappointed in the future.

Next, help your child put the report card in perspective: A report card is one of a number of ways to evaluate how a child is progressing in school. It's not the end of the world if it's not as good as it could be, nor does a straight-**A** report mean she's going to Harvard. Keep in mind that report cards are subjective assessments. Teachers assign grades based on slightly different criteria, some of which they may not even be aware of: a student has an especially nice smile, or reminds

Sample Notes to a Principal

Dear Ms. Lopez,

I am very pleased with the high level of nurturing, teaching, and child-centered atmosphere at our school. I've also been very impressed with your skills as a listener. As the mother of kindergartner, Maria Gonzalez, I would appreciate a listening ear regarding my thoughts for her first grade year.

Maria has had a wonderful year in Ms. Beam's kindergarten classroom. She has thrived academically, socially, and in her self-confidence. Ms. Beam's organized, predictable environment has supported Maria's own strong internal structure. Maria now needs to develop more flexibility and spontaneity, which will be better cultivated in a more informal classroom setting. Maria also needs to learn to negotiate independent choices within a group context. Competitive by nature, she often finds herself embroiled in "little-girl-hurt-feelings" conflicts.

I'd love to see her have a teacher who highly values and helps children focus on the early tenets of peer-conflict resolution.

Thank you for considering my concerns.

Sincerely,
Kathy Gonzalez

Dear Mr. Holcomb,

After much thought and concern, I ask that you consider the following circumstances when placing our daughter, Shelly Haynes, in fourth grade this September.

Both my parents have been very sick and each has had several hospitalizations during the past year. One parent has serious heart disease, and the other has Alzheimer's. I've had to travel to Atlanta to help them on quite a few occasions. Sometimes my departures are planned in advance, while at other times they have been sudden. We've always kept John (who is in fifth grade) and Shelly's teachers apprised of the situation.

However, my absences have been most upsetting for Shelly. I expect to continue to help my parents in the foreseeable future. Consequently, I am requesting that Shelly be placed in the loop class so she might have more stability and consistency in school during a likely disruptive next couple of years. Having the same teacher for two years in a row will most certainly be a great help.

Thank you for your consideration.

Sincerely,
Barbara Haynes

them of their least-favorite nephew. Also, consider your child's grades within context. A grade of **B** in one school or even one classroom is not necessarily the same as another. Each teacher has his own marking curve, so a lot depends on how the other kids in your child's class are doing.

No matter what you think of the overall report, try to mention something positive before you point out any problem areas.

I personally don't recommend giving children rewards, either monetary or otherwise, for getting certain grades or for a certain amount of improvement. I'd rather have a child become self-motivated. But I've known many families where a carrot seems to give a child just the push she needs to improve. You need to decide for yourself and your own child whether or not it's appropriate.

As in bank statements, errors have been known to be made with report cards. Especially as your child progresses, what shows up on her permanent record can affect her future. So if you suspect a mistake, first ask to see any pertinent tests, and so on. Then call the teacher. Also, keep all your child's report cards in her school file at home. You can keep tabs on your child's progress and spot overall trends.

I remember one memorable call I had from a parent regarding a report card. Her sixth grade daughter had received a comment—chosen from a computerized menu of comments—from her music teacher. He said, "Needs to participate more." Turns out the girl wasn't even in his class!

Regardless of whether your child did well or poorly, respond to your child's teacher when report cards come home. Take time to write a quick note of thanks. If you're pleased with your child's progress, say so. If not, ask what you could do to help.

17 KEEP A FILE FOR YOUR CHILD'S SCHOOLWORK.

Take time to review it periodically and check for patterns of steady improvement or problem areas. This is especially effective if your child "catches" you looking through her work on a regular basis. You convey how much you value education in general and her learning in particular. The actual file could be a traditional drawer with folders, a large artist's portfolio, a cardboard or plastic storage box, or even a shelf in a closet. One family I know stashes schoolwork, as well as memorabilia, in each child's backpack from the previous year.

18 UNDERSTAND THE STANDARDIZED TESTS YOUR CHILD TAKES.

You have the right to know the answers to the following questions about tests administered to your child at school:

- How often are tests given?
- Are they supplied by the state or are they bought from test publishers?
- What are the tests supposed to accomplish?
- Who chose the tests and why?
- How are the tests given?
- How are students prepared for tests?
- How are the tests scored and reported?
- How are the tests interpreted and used?
- Are the tests mandatory?

19 CAREFULLY REVIEW STANDARDIZED TEST RESULTS.

Call for explanations of anything you don't understand. This also has the effect of making the principal or teacher focus on your child individually while reviewing his test. Plus, mistakes do happen and it's pretty much up to you to spot them. Make it clear you're not questioning the results or being defensive about how well your child did. You are simply seeking information: *What is a stanine?* for example, or *What is the difference between a national norm and others?* (See the Glossary on page 209 to find out.)

20 REVIEW YOUR CHILD'S SCHOOL RECORDS.

Make it a point to check that all pertinent printed material about your child is, in fact, at school in one place. A good time to check is at the end of your child's first year in school or upon entering a new school (from elementary to middle school, from middle to high school, or when moving to a new school district). You can usually do this by phoning the school secretary. Ask whether or not any part of the school record is stored somewhere else or in some electronic form.

Then check that the applicable items from the list below are included and are accurate:

• Reports from each grade.

- Health forms.

- Standardized test results.

- Attendance records.

- Reports from school psychologist, speech therapist, reading specialist, or any other staff transcripts from other schools.

- Correspondence from social service agencies.

- Awards, honors.

- Letters of recommendation.

If there is a document you don't understand or don't recognize, question it immediately.

21 MONITOR YOUR OWN COMMENTS ABOUT SCHOOL.

Have you ever caught yourself saying something like, *I was terrible in math* or *What's the point of memorizing a bunch of dates?* or *What a dumb assignment!?* This sends a strong message to kids: You don't respect a teacher, a school, or even the value of education. It's also confusing to a child. Who should they trust? Where do their loyalties belong? So think twice before you blurt out a negative statement regarding anything to do with your child's education.

IF YOU'RE A
2–3 GRADE PARENT

Start a literacy program. **38**
Be a class parent. **32**
Lobby for an advocacy group. **89**
Start a school-community partnership. **77**
Hold a "Family Math" night. **51**

22 MAKE A POINT OF CALLING YOUR SCHOOL DISTRICT SUPERINTENDENT.

To take an active role in your child's education you need to know what's going on in your school district. A good way to do this is through the superintendent.

Unless you are on the school board or active in the PTA, you probably don't have too much to do with the superintendent because much of what he does has to do with budget and curriculum. But especially in smaller systems, superintendents will meet with parents to discuss concerns regarding their child, though it's usually best to try to talk to your child's teacher and principal first. If the problem remains unresolved then it may be time to contact the superintendent (as a matter of courtesy it's usually best to let the principal know you will be doing this).

If you have nothing specific to ask, try the following:

- What are the curriculum requirements of this school district based on?

- How does this school evaluate its teachers?

- What are the requirements for tenure in this school system?

- How does money get distributed among the schools and departments in this district?

- Are there general instruction guidelines for the teachers in this district?

- What are your goals for our schools this year?

23 TAKE YOUR CHILD TO THE LIBRARY.

Try to make this a weekly habit from the time your child is in preschool. Make going to the library a treat, whether it's for story hour, to rent a video, or to check out a pile of books on a favorite subject such as comics or animals. As soon as he can sign his own name, he should have his own library card and pick out books on his own. Keep the emphasis positive by allowing him to check out as many books as he wants and then not insisting that he finish reading them all. Overdue fines are one financial obligation I urge parents to accept gratefully.

Exploring other libraries besides the one closest to home can be an adventure you share with your child. Libraries have unique personalities, and it's fun to find out that one has a special collection of dollhouses, or another has the best storyteller around.

24 START A TELEPHONE TREE.

This activity is a geometric progression: You call two parents to discuss school issues and give them an opportunity to voice their concerns. You ask each of them to call two other parents, and so on and so forth. If you do your math, you can see how very quickly almost the whole school population will have had direct contact via telephone. What an amazingly simple way to foster a sense of school community, gather information, and lobby for involvement!

25 HELP MAKE TRANSPORTATION AND ESCORT ARRANGEMENTS.

Consider a carpool program for children or parents who can't get to after-school activities. You don't necessarily have to drive yourself—your contribution could be to organize the carpool by calling other parents. If you live in an urban setting, you could arrange for kids who stay after school and leave in the dark to have an adult accompany them home, either by walking or taking a bus or subway. In some neighborhoods, parents have established "safe routes." Participating houses, apartment buildings, or even stores post a symbol in a window to let children know that if they need help, they can knock on that door.

CHAPTER THREE

BACK TO SCHOOL

Forty-three things you can do at your child's school.

You may have already thought of doing a few of these activities, but weren't sure how to go about it. I hope this book will give you the confidence to plunge in. I know every one of these ideas has been tried by at least one parent. If they can do it, so can you!

26 MEET YOUR CHILD'S TEACHER NO LATER THAN THE FIRST DAY OF SCHOOL.

Meeting your child's teacher is not only a matter of politeness. In fact, since this first encounter will probably take place in the midst of hectic activity, you probably won't have much time to think about your manners. Here are some things you can do to make the most of this meeting:

- Keep it brief.

- Make eye contact.

- Shake his hand.

- Make a personal comment such as *It's nice to see you again,* if you already know the teacher; *Welcome to our school,* if it's a new teacher; or *We're both so excited about third grade!*

- Try to say something about your child that will stand out in the teacher's mind.

- Make a point of noting anything that strikes you as unusual or special about the teacher or the classroom.

- Suggest that you would like to follow up in a later appointment.

If you have specific thoughts or concerns regarding your child, you may want to go in a day or two before school starts or arrange to talk about it at a later date. When you meet your child's teacher the next time, assuming it's a bit more relaxed, here are some questions you might want to ask:

- How can I work with my child at home in a way that reinforces what you do in the classroom?

- How can I help you in the classroom?

- How can I help you from home?

27 DON'T MISS YOUR SCHOOL'S OPEN HOUSE NIGHT.

One of the best opportunities a parent has to evaluate a school is during an open house. There are a number of different ways you can make the most of it.

First, you have a leisurely opportunity to really check out your child's environment: the place he spends umpteen hours a week. From the moment you walk in the door, observe carefully. Have a mental checklist:

- Is student work hanging everywhere in the classroom? Or is it overly neat and tidy?

- How are desks or seats arranged? Are they in traditional rows, blocks of four, or circular?

- Are there plenty of stimulating posters, quotes, books, and other materials?

- Is it cheerful, light, and comfortable?

- Is there a place for children to put their jackets, backpacks, and lunches? Or do they get jumbled up on the floor?

Try to make a point of introducing yourself to each teacher and administrator there. Start with a general comment or questions to set the tone and telegraph the fact that you are interested in the whole class or school. Then you might move on to more specific concerns about your own child. But only do this after the more formal, public presentation. There's nothing less effective, not to mention rude, than a parent interrupting a teacher's carefully prepared description of the year's science curriculum with a complaint about how the other kids are making Sammy feel dumb or a question on why Melissa didn't get a better grade on her last quiz.

During any general question and answer session, you might ask the following:

- What are your goals or expectations for this class?

- Can you describe the year's curriculum?

- How would you characterize the personality of this group so far?

- What's your policy on homework?

Another benefit of going to an open house is the opportunity to meet other parents. Especially as your child gets older, you may have fewer chances to get to know his classmates' parents. So don't be shy, go ahead and search them out. Forming a network of involved parents is essential in forming an effective school/parent partnership.

An equally important part of attending an open house is having a debriefing with your child afterwards. Share your impressions in as positive a way as you can and ask your child about something—anything—you noticed. This reinforces the message that you are interested in education and that you care about your child.

28 SIGN UP FOR ONE FIELD TRIP EACH SCHOOL YEAR.

Teachers almost always need more adult chaperones when they take kids off-campus, and going on field trips is a tried-and-true form of parent involvement. But there are ways to get more out of a field trip—and to provide more help too. Try to choose when you volunteer based on the type of trip rather than on the most convenient date. If you go with your child's class to a passive performance, for example, you'll be doing a lot of shushing and shepherding but not much else. Pick more interactive trips, such as a walking tour of an historic area, a museum visit, or a nature center. You'll probably be divided into small groups and get to relate to your child and a few other students more directly. You'll be able to ask the kids questions, and learn what they're learning. No doubt this kind of participation requires more energy on your part—it's not easy guiding six rambunctious eight-year-olds through a museum (hint: have jumping jack breaks!)—but the payoff is usually worth it.

29 GIVE A TALK ON YOUR PROFESSION OR AREA OF EXPERTISE TO STUDENTS.

I encourage anybody with a skill, hobby, or interest to teach it. You don't have to worry about classroom discipline because the teacher is there to keep order. A teacher will come to me and say, "A parent has a job in the stock market. I have a second grade class. He'd like to come and talk about stock markets. What do you think?" I say, "Great! Let him come. Talk a little bit before about what to do. Set it up with him. But bring him in." This is particularly helpful if what you do fits in with the curriculum.

I know one Illinois mother, a published poet, who volunteered to talk to her son's fourth grade class during their poetry unit. After she agreed, the first thing she did was to arrange a convenient time with the teacher. She made a point of asking when the kids would be most alert and exactly how long the teacher thought they could pay attention. Given this information, she planned her presentation to last about twenty minutes, allowing ten minutes extra for the children's questions and fifteen minutes for a student activity. She brought plenty of show and tell: her notebooks, where she wrote by hand; her typed drafts with all the revisions; and books with the final, published version. It was a way for the students to see clearly how much work went into a single poem and that poetry wasn't a magical process. Then she had them try writing their own poems, while she went around the room chatting individually to the kids who were having trouble getting started or were eager to show her their creations.

Another mother, in Nevada, called her son's first grade teacher and asked if she could give a short talk the day before Veterans Day on why we tried to remember certain people at this time. The teacher hadn't thought of doing anything and welcomed the suggestion. The kids enjoyed making little flags as the activity.

So, don't wait to be asked—volunteer.

30 DECORATE!

Schools aren't usually places of physical beauty or splendor, but they *can* be cheerful, inviting, and friendly looking. When the parents at P.S. 75 painted all the doors throughout the building, it made a dramatic, instant difference in morale. Teachers, parents, and especially the children seemed to visibly brighten as they saw the beautiful designs beckoning them to enter. The great thing about decorating is that it doesn't have to take much money. With paint, sweat equity, and creativity, parents can transform a school in a relatively short period of time.

Start by taking a stroll around the campus. Try to look at the smallest details and also notice the biggest eyesores. What single change would be most effective? Fixing the broken windows? Painting the dingy hallways a light, bright color? Planting greenery in the barren dirt patch? If you tackle the worst part first, it will be the most gratifying—and inspire others to pitch in.

Naturally, you can't just show up with a paint bucket and dive in. Every school has a different protocol. Sometimes the simplest approach is to go straight to the principal with a concrete suggestion of what you'd like to do. If she can't give you a green light on the spot, she will be able to tell you who you do need to contact. Once you have some sort of official approval, you can solicit help from as many other parents as you think necessary. It's always effective to include children too. That way parents can spend time with their kids and the kids feel a sense of ownership of their school. The

school will love you for this kind of contribution—
and see you as a positive partner.

31 VOLUNTEER TO BE AN IN-CLASS ASSISTANT FOR ONE HOUR A WEEK.

Even if you work, you probably could manage to
squeeze in one hour a week at your child's school.
If your schedule is flexible, all the better. What can
you do? Start, of course, by asking the teacher
what specific tasks could most use your help. She
may be so unaccustomed to a parent asking how to
help, though, that she needs some suggestions. You
could then suggest a variety of options such as the
following: singing with the children, playing an
instrument for them, reading them a story, helping
prepare a snack, listening to the children read,
drilling them on basic math facts, or editing stories
children have written.

Assistants in older grades might help reorganize
classroom materials, file student work, or tutor
writing.

32 BE A CLASS PARENT.

Being a class parent is one traditional way of being directly involved with your child's education. Many parents choose to do this in the early years of elementary school, because it's a good way to see firsthand what goes on in the classroom, especially when your child is too young to communicate it well.

If you know you'd like to be a class parent, or room parent as they are sometimes called, but you don't know when is the best time for you to pitch in, here are some ways to think about it:

- In the child's early years, class parents have more tasks and spend more time on their duties than later on. If you are busy but would like to serve in the classroom at some point, maybe waiting is best for you.

- As your child gets older, she may tend to share her daily experiences with you less, so being a class parent is a good way to keep abreast of what's going on.

- If your goal is service, it is probably best to wait until the later grades, because parent interest tends to wane as children get older.

IF YOU'RE A
FULL-TIME WORKING PARENT

Start a telephone tree. **24**

Host a field trip at your workplace. **83**

Write a grant proposal. **74**

Attend school board meetings. **72**

Sign up for one field trip per school year. **28**

Usually deciding when to be a class parent can be based on your child's development—when they seem to need you around most, when they seem distant—or when you feel you can make the commitment. There is also a range of responsibility and kinds of tasks that class parents take on. For example, in elementary school, a class parent may be expected to:

- Organize class picnics.
- Help with holiday or birthday parties.
- Aid in the classroom.
- Assist in making classroom materials.
- Collect money for class gifts to teachers.

- Attend class field trips.
- Collect money for book orders.

When all these seemingly small tasks are done by a parent, the teacher is freed from what I call *administrivia*.

In high school, the tasks are usually fewer and farther between, but they can be more time-consuming. A class parent may be asked to:

- Schedule parent-teacher conferences.
- Attend school dances or functions.
- Chaperone school trips.
- Arrange graduation festivities.

33 RUN A NATURE PROGRAM.

Nature programs can be fairly basic or quite elaborate. For instance, in the elementary school of Hastings-on-Hudson, New York, each Friday parents take small groups of children on nature walks during the school day. The school happens to be located adjacent to a woods with a pond, so a virtual goldmine of natural phenomena is at their doorstep.

Gale Rosskoff, a Ph.D. microbiologist with two children in the North Caldwell, New Jersey, school system, started an even more ambitious program. She believes this generation of kids will be making critical decisions about the environment, and they're not being well-prepared. According to Rosskoff, environmental education should begin quite early since people are unlikely to protect something they don't know much about. Kids have a natural curiosity when they're young, and aside from her own motives, Rosskoff thought a nature program would be a lot of fun for kids, as well as a great starting point for writing projects and math lessons, among other things.

So Rosskoff approached the principal of her children's elementary school and asked permission to take the kids on a field trip on school property. She set about creating a curriculum for a science class the way she thought it should—and could—be. She took her involvement seriously from the start because she knew that if she were going to be taking time out of the school day the program had to be top-notch. She did lots of research and contacted the New Jersey Audubon Society and the Liberty Science Center. She found a framework for the kind of program she wanted to build in a book called *Bridges to the Natural World* published by the New Jersey Audubon Society.

Once she had her curriculum together, she approached the principal and the superintendent for their approval, which she received. She also went to the PTA with her plan to make sure there were no objections. Not only did they support her program but they offered funding if she needed it.

The surprising thing was that she didn't need funding. She gathered thirteen other parents who each volunteered an hour-and-a-half of their time once a week for eight weeks. This enabled each class in the small elementary school to take the field trip twice a year. She posted the dates when the class would be held, so teachers could sign their classes up if they were interested. There was 100 percent participation.

Classes were an hour-and-a-half long, and were made up of between sixteen to twenty kids and four adults. For the first half hour of the sessions, she would talk to the group, and maybe tell a story or ask some questions on what they already knew about that day's topic. Then they would break into four small groups and work on that day's assignment. Each leader had a lesson plan for the day's activity, for example, a scavenger hunt: Each child had to find five different-shaped leaves, five different types of insects, and so on. Then the class returned to the classroom for a related arts and crafts project. For the scavenger hunt each child made a "Tree Book" by pasting the leaves into blank paper books.

The Nature Program ran for three years with no help from the schools, except for $100 they supplied. Rosskoff was able to demonstrate that it doesn't have to cost a lot of money to do really exciting, interesting projects. In fact, with a little creativity and resourcefulness it doesn't have to cost anything at all. For example, during a unit on flowers, Rosskoff planned to have the kids each dissect a flower, find the embryonic seeds inside, and glue each part of the flower's anatomy separately on a sheet of paper. The only problem was finding 250 flowers. So she started at the most obvious place—where she buys her flowers. She went to her local supermarket (where she is a regular) and asked if they could supply her with sixty flowers a week for four weeks and they said yes without hesitation. Another time, she was planning to make binoculars out of toilet paper tubes and yarn for the kids to use, but she felt a little funny about taking them used out of people's bathrooms. So she called a tissue paper company and asked if they could supply her with some cardboard tubing. They were glad to.

The only hitches Rosskoff encountered while she ran the program were not financial at all. The first was finding help. While volunteers are great, they are also not required to be there, so she was sometimes left without help at the last minute. She recommends that if you will be relying on help from other parents or community volunteers, make sure that you have enough or too many helpers.

The other problem Rosskoff encountered was parents who heard through the grapevine about her program and called the board of education asking, *Who is this Gale Rosskoff to take it into her own hands to rebuild the Science Program?* She immediately contacted a board member and informed him of her qualifications and motivations. She realized that though she had gotten approval from the PTA, principal, and superintendent, she hadn't made sure the administration advertised their support and notified parents that their children would be participating in this program. Be sure to be sensitive to all constituents within the system when introducing change.

Though North Caldwell and Hastings-on-Hudson are suburban towns, the ideas and methods behind Rosskoff's program can be put to work most anywhere. Most urban areas have parks or other accessible green space. Rosskoff says there's even science in unlikely places such as concrete, where you can find ant colonies, tough little plants, and microscopic life forms in puddles.

34 START AN AFTER-SCHOOL CLUB.

Find out what's missing in your child's school day. Could your child use more exercise? Teach karate. More hands-on art? Do crafts projects. More socializing? Supervise a games period. A parents' organization such as the PTA can sponsor a series of "clubs" and even charge a small fee, but you could just as easily do it on an individual basis with less red tape. Start by checking with your school's principal. Reassure him that it wouldn't require any of his time or budget. Then ask permission to send a flyer home with each child describing the club. Have fun!

35 START A SCHOOL NEWSPAPER OR LITERARY MAGAZINE.

I know of a parent who did this primarily to offer her gifted child more stimulation at school—but it turned out the entire school benefited and it is still going strong years after her child graduated. Here's how it worked:

Judy McQuistion, of Irvington, New York, and her friend, Robin Berry, first made an appointment with the principal, Joe Rodriguez. McQuistion, a preschool teacher, and Berry, a freelance journalist, presented their idea in an open-ended way, inviting Rodriguez to help them decide whether to involve the PTA, which grade levels to include, and when to schedule the activity. Together they worked out a simple plan. Rodriguez had a few hundred dollars from the PTA he could allocate directly to the newspaper. That was enough to cover the costs of having it printed and collated. He suggested they start with mostly fifth graders and a few fourth graders who could apprentice. Rodriguez arranged with his teachers for the two parents to visit each fourth and fifth grade class to present the idea of starting a school paper and to ask who would be interested. They scheduled the activity to meet twice a week during lunch time, because that fit into their own work schedules well. Kids already involved in two or more other activities, such as band or the school play, were automatically eliminated. That left a manageable-enough number of fifteen students who wanted to participate.

Rodriguez found an available classroom and they were off and running. They gave the kids a short course in basic journalism, and then encouraged them to make the major decisions themselves:

- They named the paper. *The Bull Dog's Bark* is what they came up with, as the bull dog was the sports team mascot.

- They chose the stories they'd write. The front page story in the first issue was about the construction of an addition planned for the school. Students reported on each classroom's activities and themes as well.

- They planned the special columns. Sports, TV and movie reviews, profiles of school personnel, classifieds, and original cartoons became regular features. In addition, they had a question in each issue that everyone could respond to by placing an answer in a box in the school's lobby. The following issue would print the responses.

- They assigned each story.

The two parent volunteers did the "typesetting" on a computer, but only after the articles were edited by the student staff. The kids also did the layout and paste-up for each issue before McQuistion took it to the printer. Finally, the newspaper team distributed the paper to every student in the school.

With Rodriguez's full support and the students taking on a lot of responsibility, the paper was not only a success, it really didn't take much of McQuistion's time after the initial planning.

36 START A MEDIATION PROGRAM.

Grades 4–6 are when fights, both physical and verbal, are prone to break out. Educators for Social Responsibility in Cambridge, Massachusetts, have a lot of information about teaching mediation. They suggest students use lunch break as a time to learn conflict-resolution skills. A trained parent steps in only if the situation gets out of hand.

We had a mediation program in my last school, and I loved it. Although it's particularly needed in urban settings, all students benefit from learning active listening skills and how to not take sides in an argument. So we're thinking of starting mediation here in Rye Brook. If we do, there are not enough school personnel to supervise it, especially in the initial phase of setting it up. We will rely on parents.

37 BEGIN A PUBLISHING CENTER.

This is definitely one of the more ambitious ideas in this book. But when parents establish a publishing center in a school, the benefits seem to ripple outwards for quite a ways. If you can gather together enough other parents, no one person has to shoulder too much responsibility.

What is a publishing center? It's a way to "publish" student writing in a more lasting form. Especially effective for elementary school children, it allows them to feel a lot of pride in their work when they see it typed, bound, and covered with fabric-over-cardboard. You can set up your center in a corner of a classroom or take over the entire computer lab periodically. In some schools, parents have even been able to obtain rooms solely for use as a publishing center.

Teachers send students one by one to go over production of their work with a parent volunteer during the publishing center hours. They tell the parent what title they'd like, how the dedication should read, whether they want to illustrate it, and which fabric pattern they want for their cover. The parent typesets the story or poem on a computer, either at school or at home, and prints it out. If the child is illustrating a book, the parent lays out each page to leave room for a drawing. After that, the adult makes a cover, using donated fabric, and presents the finished work to the author. To hear a child shouting, "My book, look at my book!" is truly a rich reward.

At one suburban K–5 school, two first grade teachers approached parents asking for help in setting up a publishing center. Both teachers and parents visited a neighboring school with a well-run center to see how they did it. After several organizational meetings, they spoke with the principal and reported that they felt ready to begin. He provided space in part of a special education classroom for the first year, and the publishing center opened three days a week from 10 a.m. to 2 p.m. Students signed up on a sheet posted outside the room and teachers sent them to the center as the schedule permitted. A total of about twenty parent volunteers now work at this center. Finished books are displayed in the school library, and families can even order additional copies as gifts. In addition to short fiction books, the center also offers poetry published in individual frames.

One reason the center has been so successful is that it's extremely well organized. There are printed forms and instructions for each step of the process, beginning with the editor/binder training form all the way through an additional copy order form. See pages 84–85 and pages 236–238 for examples.

Here's what you'll need to start a publishing center:

- As many adult volunteers as possible, with a minimum of five.

- Access to computers and printers.

- A place to meet with the children to go over their writing during school hours.
- High-quality paper.
- Heavy cardboard, rulers, rubber cement, masking tape.
- Plenty of fabric or some other material suitable for a book cover.
- Binding supplies: needles, thread, scissors.

The following are nice but not absolutely necessary at first:

- Ironing board for fabric.
- Baggies to put each book in at various stages of production.
- Publishing center bookplates to stick on inside front cover.
- Xacto knives for making frames for individual poems.

Manuscript Cover/Instruction Form

Student's Name   Date

Teacher's Name   Grade

Title of Book

Book Size   4 1/2" x 6"   6" x 9"   7" x 11"

Dedication

Special Instructions

Volunteer's Name   Edited   Typed   Proofread

Library Display Sign-Up Sheet

Would you like to see your published book displayed in the school library? We will display it for two weeks and give the whole school a chance to enjoy it!

_____
Name

_____
Teacher

_____
Date book was given to student

_____
Date book was put on display

_____
Date book must be returned to student

Library Display Reminder Note

Dear _____,

Once you have shared your illustrated book with your family and friends, please bring it back to DOWS LANE PUBLISHING CENTER so that we can put it on display in the library. We really look forward to seeing your finished work!

Sincerely,
The Dows Lane Publishing Center Staff

38 START A LITERACY PROGRAM.

At my school in Rye Brook, New York, a parent heard about a literacy program called "Wee Deliver," sponsored by the U.S. Postal Service. They give a kit with an actual mailbox to a school, which becomes a small town where each corridor is a street, each classroom a house with a number. Children have their own addresses in school and they send mail to each other. They take a little civil-service exam and become postmasters. Children learn how to sort, how to stack, and how to plan, and they deliver mail daily to other classes and even from outside.

We couldn't have this program if this parent wasn't willing to do all the work. It took her a lot of time to organize it, to modify the civil-service exam, to have a meeting with teachers to explain the program in hopes they would endorse it. Once you train the children, the program has an adult postmaster that does ongoing supervision. It's only the setup that takes the time, and that's what this parent was willing to give. She has a job outside the home, so she couldn't work in the school on a regular basis. But she could offer a tremendous amount of creativity and organizational skills. Today, when you walk around the school, you see the result as signs proclaim Wellness Way, Creativity Lane, Red Hat Road, Boardwalk, and Locker Lane.

39 PREPARE AHEAD FOR A PARENT-TEACHER CONFERENCE.

Most schools hold parent-teacher conferences once or twice a year. (If your school does not, make a point of requesting them.) You might not have a lot of choice as to when you can meet your child's teacher, but try to be as accommodating as possible, even if it means working late or skipping a lunch hour. This is one of the best opportunities you have to give and get vital information. In my school, we encourage parents to provide "insider's secrets" by having them fill out a questionnaire (see pages 92–95) before the conference. We find it gives us a tremendous advantage in understanding their children.

A productive parent-teacher conference should give you the chance to:

- Make sure your goals and the teacher's goals are in line.

- Know what's being expected of your child.

- Help your child to meet those expectations.

- Find out where your child is in relationship to the rest of the class.

- Approach the teacher with ease in case of a future problem.

Before the conference, talk to your child! Let her know you are having this conference. Ask if she has any special concerns or questions she'd like you to discuss with her teacher. Often children will volunteer information at this point that they've held back. You might ask: *Do you feel as if you're challenged enough in this class or subject? What do you like best about it? Is there any part of the class you dislike? How are you getting along with the other kids? What's the homework load like for you? Are you comfortable and happy with where you're sitting in class? Can you see and hear well enough? If there was just one thing you'd want your teacher to know about you, what would it be?*

Talk to your spouse about your agenda for the conference. Even if you're both attending, it's a good idea to review any specific items you want to cover ahead of time. If only one of you is going, the other one can help clarify what you want to get out of the meeting.

Either mentally or in writing, figure out what you want to tell and ask the teacher, in order of importance. That way, if you run out of time, you'll at least have covered the most essential information.

Here are some sample questions:

• Is my child adjusting to this grade?

- Does my child seem to be working up to her capacity? Is she at grade level, above, or below?

- Have you noticed any strengths or weaknesses in my child?

- Is she participating much?

- What is your homework policy? How about tests and quizzes?

- What sorts of long-term projects will you be assigning this year?

- How does my child get along with the other children? Have there been any problems?

- Does my child show any special interests or talents?

- What can I do to help you help my child?

- How and when do you like to be contacted? Is the telephone or a note better?

- What should we expect next year (for second semester conferences)? What can you tell us about next year's curriculum and teachers?

40 MAKE THE MOST OF YOUR PARENT-TEACHER CONFERENCES.

Please, whatever you do, if you must cancel or reschedule a conference, let the teacher know as soon as possible. Although this might seem like the most basic common courtesy, I can't tell you how many times teachers have complained to me about parent no-shows. Not only does this inconvenience and annoy your child's teacher, it also ultimately hurts your child.

Along the same lines, be as punctual as possible for your conference. Usually conferences are scheduled so closely together that one late parent can throw off many peoples' days.

At the conference, begin by telling your child's teacher something upbeat such as *Matthew came home raving about the terrarium project.* This kind of comment telegraphs instantly to the teacher that you are supportive of her efforts on your child's behalf. But that doesn't mean you can't be assertive in voicing your questions and concerns. The ideal conference is a conversation between parent and teacher, not a monologue where all you do is listen for twenty minutes. Let the teacher know what you've observed about your child's behavior regarding homework, adjustment, emotional health, fatigue level—anything you think might help the teacher understand your whole child better.

If a teacher doesn't offer to show you your child's work, ask to see it and ask the teacher to comment on it.

After the conference, report back to your child with enthusiasm and pride. Try to put a positive spin on whatever the teacher said about your child. For example, if you found out he is "disruptive," ask why he seems to have so much energy at school. Instead of saying, *Ms. Hanson thinks you aren't working hard enough,* you could say, *Ms. Hanson and I agreed that you are really smart. We know you can do even better next semester.* It's helpful to say something specific about your child's teacher, too, to hammer home the fact that you are all on the same side: *I thought Mr. Walters made a terrific suggestion for how you could improve your writing* or *I was impressed by how much Ms. Snell seems to care about you and all her students.*

A follow-up note is a good way to cement your relationship with the teacher. You can take the opportunity to repeat in writing any action steps you and she discussed or to let her know anything you forgot to mention at the conference.

Parent Conference Questionnaires

VERSION 1

Dear Parent:

This letter is to confirm your appointment for a conference on _____ from _____ to _____ . The questions below may help you prepare for your conference:

1. How does your child feel about school?

2. Has your child had any health problems that we should know about? (Sight, hearing, allergies, diet, and so on.)

3. How does your child accept responsibility at home?

4. How does your child spend his time outside of school?

5. What are your child's hobbies, special interests, or abilities?

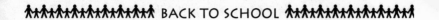

6. What types of books does your child choose to read at home?

7. How does your child get along with other children? With adults?

8. What concerns about school does your child share with you?

9. In what ways can we work together to make this a successful year for your child?

VERSION 2

(With examples of a parent's answers.)

Child's Name: Claudia Silbert

Conference Questionnaire: Our conferences are only 15 minutes long. To use that time most effectively, I would like you to answer the following questions so that I can answer your questions at the conference. Please return this page ASAP.

Thanks,

Martha Nelson

1. What do you want your child to accomplish this year?

   Listening skills, focusing, training, numbers, learning the computer, and also social interaction.

2. What questions do you have concerning your child that you would like to have answered at the conference?

   Adjusting to first grade; her speech.

3. What questions does your child have that you would

like to talk about at the conference?

Does she have a speech problem?

Please return this questionnaire with your child as soon as possible. Thank you.

41 GO TO GAMES AND CONCERTS.

This might seem a bit obvious—what parent wouldn't want to see a child running down a field or singing heart out?—but it always amazes me how many parents do not, cannot, or will not be there for a child. Usually there is a way. If you can't make an evening event, perhaps there is a dress rehearsal you could sneak into, for example. No matter what your child says, especially in middle or high school, chances are he will feel your presence deeply. Be sensitive to your child: If he is self-conscious, you can stay quietly on the sidelines. If he's more extroverted, your loud cheers might be welcome.

Another possibility is attending school events *with* your child when he is not performing or playing.

IF YOU'RE A
4–5 GRADE PARENT

Be a school aide, lunchroom, playground, or bus
aide. **45**

Give a talk on your profession or area of expertise
to students. **29**

Begin a publishing center. **37**

Start a mediation program. **36**

Put on a talent show. **63**

42 SHARE A COLLECTION OR A CUSTOM.

If you have a special collection of some kind, see
whether your school would like you to display it
and give a talk on it. The collection could include
anything from stamps and coins to birdhouses and
dolls. Collections can be a marvelous way of teaching a little history. Sharing your enthusiasm might
spark a child's interest in starting a collection of his
own.

You can apply the same idea to a special family
story that reveals cultural values and customs.

Parents from other countries can be elevated and honored instead of feeling self-conscious about accents or unusual clothing.

43 GET INVOLVED IN AN AFTER-SCHOOL TUTORING PROGRAM.

Olga Ferrer has four kids in the Cleveland, Ohio, school district. She has been involved in the schools since the oldest (now seventeen) was in kindergarten, most recently in an after-school tutoring program. The tutors in this program are teachers, but volunteers like Ferrer have been sent to educational conferences and meetings to keep up with the latest strategies and standards, which they then report back to faculty.

Regina Mans started volunteering when her daughter was in the Atenville Elementary School in rural Harts, West Virginia. When she was a girl, moms stayed at home "where they were supposed to be." But once she came into the building she felt much more comfortable. She wasn't working outside the home, so she spent most of her time at the school, and heard right away when the position of volunteer coordinator opened up. Teachers started talking about the need for a tutoring program for children who were having academic trouble, and Mans jumped right in with help.

Mans galvanized parents to arrange for any child who requests a tutor to be paired up with one. Most of the tutors in the after-school program are high school students who came through Atenville Elementary. The rest are parents. Since it is a small town where everybody knows everyone else, parent volunteers match the students and tutors according to compatibility and need. The program runs for an hour after school or in the evenings once a week. Up to sixty-five kindergartners through sixth-graders receive help at the program's peak. When a problem arose with transportation, the program moved temporarily to a local church at the center of town and within walking distance of most families' homes.

44 VISIT ON VISITING DAY.

If your school has a day each year for parents to sit in on their children's classes, make it a priority to attend. You will get to see how teachers interact with students and how students interact with each other. It's the best and only way to get a handle on exactly what your child's day is like.

If your school doesn't have a formal open classroom day once a year, get together with other parents to request this. It's an invaluable way to take charge of your child's education.

Meanwhile, if you are going to visit a school, let your child know ahead of time you will be coming into her class. You don't want to disrupt a class by surprising her.

If your child is in middle school or high school, there is a good chance she will try to convince you to skip it. She will read you the riot act, tell you not a single other parent is going, and insist that you will ruin her life if you show up. Ignore this. Calmly state that checking on her education is one of the most important parts of being a parent and that it's non-negotiable. If, in fact, you *are* one of the few parents who attend visiting day, try to lobby to get others to go next year. Call the principal, mention your concern to teachers, offer to help better promote and advertise this opportunity.

Once inside the classroom:

- Observe the attitude and energy level of the students. Are they attentive, engaged, focused, eager? Or do they seem bored, tired, and unruly?

- Check out the overall atmosphere of the classroom. Is it cheerful, bright, and airy? Or is it tense and uncomfortable?

- Notice whether students have assigned seats or free choice. What is the arrangement of desks?

- Watch student/teacher and student/student interactions. You can check out art work, assignments, posters, and so on more carefully at a nighttime open house, but this is your only chance to observe your child.

- How much participation is there? Do girls and boys participate equally?

- Listen to everything the teacher says and how she says it. Is she patient when she answers questions? Does she ask the students "why" a lot? Does she offer plenty of positive affirmation rather than put-downs?

- Jot down some specific questions you can ask your child later about what you saw and heard. For example, *What was the answer to that brain teaser Mrs. Roth gave you?* Or, *When Mr. Levine talked about the Peace Corps did you understand what he meant?* This is another good way to follow up and demonstrate your involvement.

45 BE A SCHOOL AIDE, LUNCHROOM, PLAYGROUND, OR BUS AIDE.

Becoming an aide is a good alternative for those who aren't quite ready or willing to be a full-time teacher. In some school districts, aides are hired to help teach in a regular classroom setting under a regular teacher's direct supervision. Usually this is a budget-cutting measure, but it does allow a parent to gain hands-on experience helping students with reading, computer skills, or taking them to the library. Other types of aides are meant to relieve teachers of more mundane duties such as supervising a cafeteria or playground. These positions are always part-time and therefore particularly good for parents who have younger children and don't want to work outside the home full-time. Although they are traditionally low paying, aide jobs do let a parent have very direct contact with their child's school environment. Imagine, for example, being able to watch how your child behaves during recess or at lunch. Not only that, you get to see how the whole school "culture" works and put your child into that context. Also, once you have several years of experience as an aide, often you are in a perfect position to move up to substitute teacher or another staff position.

Jose Payan is a classroom aide in his daughter's second grade class at Hueco Elementary School in El Paso, Texas. At the beginning of the year, the teacher asked for volunteers so she would have more time to spend with each of her seventeen students as they learned reading, writing, and math.

Payan goes to the school each day after he gets off work (around noon) and spends about an hour-and-a-half in the classroom. Usually it's just him and the teacher, and he helps out by going around the classroom and checking students' work, answering questions, and helping them with essays and other writing assignments. He brings in small science projects to do with the kids—one week he brought in some magnets and taught them about polar opposites, compasses, and how the attraction works.

Payan didn't know what to expect when he first started volunteering—he just walked in and did what was asked of him. But he says it wasn't too hard, and any parent could do it.

46 BECOME A TEACHER.

This is certainly the ultimate in parental involvement! The world always needs more terrific teachers, and who knows, maybe you'd make a fantastic teacher. Of course, this is not an idea to take lightly. If you think you might be interested, ask yourself the following questions:

- Do I like being in front of an audience?
- Am I a "people" person?
- Am I patient?
- Do I want to keep learning?
- Am I enthusiastic, energetic, and self-confident?
- Do I have a well-developed sense of humor?
- Can I adapt to new situations?
- How would I feel if a student challenged me in class?
- How do I feel about discipline?

If your answers suggest you'd be well-suited to this critical profession, pursue it further with more in-depth research. You can start by calling your state department of education office to find out exactly what your state requires for teacher certification. In general, states require a high school and bachelor's degree, a certain minimum of teaching courses, some experience teaching, and passing standardized tests.

Meanwhile, you might check out the requirements for substitute teaching as a sort of tryout—substitutes often don't have to have as much special training.

47 HELP OUT IN THE SCHOOL LIBRARY.

In elementary schools, library assistants can read to young children, shelve and catalogue books, tidy magazine collections, create displays, and check books out. For middle and high schools, a library assistant might help students find research materials. Or they may mean the difference between keeping the library open after school hours or not. One high school I know has parents volunteer for two hours once a month to make the library available to students from three to five o'clock. Why not ask your school librarian what the current hours are? If they seem limited, you could volunteer to organize a group of parents to extend the hours.

48 DEVELOP AN ARTS APPRECIATION UNIT.

Linda McCabe volunteers through the Art Appreciation Program in North Caldwell, New Jersey. Developed over fourteen years ago for kindergartners through sixth graders, it's still going strong. Today, twelve parents get together monthly to choose an artist to present. Each parent goes into two or three classrooms to introduce the artist of

IF YOU'RE A
6–8 GRADE PARENT

Visit on visiting day. **44**

Clip and send articles of possible interest to your child's school. **3**

Offer carpentry skills. **49**

Become a parent liaison. **68**

Ask about your child's day. **5**

the month to the class. They bring prints or posters to show the kids, and begin a discussion about the artist's life. They talk about his personality and interests, trying to highlight aspects the kids can relate to. For example, when Norman Rockwell was the artist of the month, they talked about his sense of humor and patriotism. Then they turned to his painting, and asked questions like, *Where's the light source in this picture?* or, *Where does your eye get drawn?* Sometimes with the older kids, they'll look at works from different phases of the artist's career and compare how his style has changed.

Occasionally they'll host a contest, putting up three different pictures and challenging the kids to figure out which is, say, a Norman Rockwell painting. The winners of the contest get their pictures taken and posted on the Art Appreciation Wall near the school office.

Finally, the kids do a project related to that month's artist. For Norman Rockwell, the kids were asked to draw a picture of something that was important to them. A couple of the moms in the program had the pictures printed as note cards, and sold them to parents. Parents had a permanent, practical keepsake of their children's work and money was raised for the program's future projects.

For McCabe, the few hours a month she spends on the Art Appreciation Program give her a chance to keep up with her lifelong interest in art and to be involved in the education of each of her four children. She says, "It's important to be involved in your school district. Not only does it make your kids happy, but it helps you stay in touch with what's going on in the schools, what programs are good, what the potential problems are, how the other kids in your child's class are developing."

49 OFFER CARPENTRY SKILLS.

Every school has continuous maintenance work. It's hard to get anything "extra" constructed or fixed in addition to the basics. This is where a parent can literally offer hands-on help. Once a parent in my New York City school asked, "Why are the bulletin boards so high? My kid can't see her own work!" The custodian said, "There's no way I have time to lower all the bulletin boards." So I went back to the parent, who is a writer, and said, "How about you?" He said, "I'd be willing. I have time on my hands." So the parent came in and nailed wood strips on the walls for bulletin boards so we could hang children's artwork a little bit lower. He and the custodian worked together with a few other parents. He came in the morning and he did it over a two-month period. We paid for the materials, and we got the job done together.

50 START A SPECIAL BRANCH OF YOUR PARENTS ORGANIZATION.

In Birmingham, Alabama, parents formed the Wenonah Elementary's Active Volunteers to make home visits, loan computers to take home, give seminars, and supplement the efforts of the PTA in a variety of areas of school life. The group assigns regular responsibilities to its participants, including substitute teaching, to enable teachers to visit other schools for curriculum inspiration.

51 HOLD A "FAMILY MATH" NIGHT.

This wonderful, well-established program, begun in California, offers six sessions of hands-on math activities for parents and their children to do together at school, but in the evening. Although the sessions provide solid math lessons, they seem more like playing than problem solving. For example, one session involves Lego bricks. A parent in Berkeley, California, remembers going to a "Family Math Night" with her first grade son as an eye-opening experience. She realized there were so many ways she could be "doing math" with her child during real-world, real-life time: at the grocery store, in the bank, while cooking a recipe.

To arrange a "Family Math Night" in your school, see page 189.

52 ORGANIZE A SATURDAY MORNING WORK PARTY.

Invite parents to come to school and help teachers rearrange their classrooms, prepare lessons, assemble kits for science activities, or plant a garden. The possibilities are endless: The point is to find a need and offer to fill it. Serving coffee and donuts doesn't hurt either.

Parents at the Springhurst Elementary School in Dobbs Ferry, New York, were notified that the antiquated playground was being demolished. They got together a small army to build a unique playground in one weekend. Designed by one of the parents, it featured castle-like structures, catwalks, turrets, and all the nooks and crannies that children dream of. Its reputation as one of the world's best playgrounds spread quickly and soon kids from neighboring communities were welcomed to use it after school and on weekends.

A few years later, this special playground was destroyed by arson. Once again parents came to the rescue, mobilizing immediately to make yet another fabulous playground rise like a phoenix so that another generation of children can play in endlessly imaginative ways.

53 INTRODUCE "ODYSSEY OF THE MIND."

Started in 1978 and originally designed only for the "gifted," the Odyssey of the Mind School Program teaches children creative problem solving. Student participants then present their solutions at Odyssey of the Mind competitions, where they are ranked by how well they solved the problem. One of the problems children may be asked to work on, for example, is to "create and present a humorous performance where an inanimate object comes to life. The performance will include a team-created poem or song and team-created music. In addition, all of the team's props must fit within a limited space. The creative emphases of this problem are on the humor of the performance, how the object is portrayed as being alive, and the poem or song."

Any school can buy these materials, which also include rules, limitations, requirements, and an explanation of how the project will be scored. But it takes extra personnel to run the program. In my current school parents who have time volunteer, and each one is a coach for one group of five or six kids of mixed ability. The parents supervise each group during lunch time twice a week for an eight-week period, so it's manageable. We could have as many groups as we have parent volunteers.

We play down the competition part. We don't hand out trophies. We want the children to have the experience of being happy in a group creating something using prior knowledge but applying it in creative ways. (See page 200 for information.)

54 PARTICIPATE IN A PUBLIC SPEAKING PROGRAM.

The gifted and talented department faculty at one school recruits parent volunteers to come in and coach fifth and sixth grade students on public speaking. The volunteers offer as much time as they are able, and take students out of class for fifteen-minute periods to tutor them. A public speaking program is a great, low-stress way to offer kids an extra learning experience, one they will most definitely be able to use throughout their lives, from the time they interview for college to the moment they run for their first office. Parents don't necessarily have to have formal public speaking backgrounds—if they've ever served on a committee, given a presentation at work, or a toast at a reception, chances are they have enough skills and common sense to help a youngster. Of course if there happens to be someone in the community who is a public relations consultant, all the better.

55 START AN ORCHESTRA.

Although many schools still have bands, fewer seem to offer students the chance to play in an orchestra. While there is some overlap in which instruments each includes, a band leaves out kids who want to play, say, the violin or cello. Also, there is a completely different repertoire of music an orchestra can play.

A violinist I know is also a mother. Frustrated that her daughter's middle school did not have an orchestra, she approached the school board with the suggestion that it consider funding such music. What she did *not* do is complain loudly and negatively or just grumble to other parents. She quietly wrote a complete, solid, well-researched proposal for the board, which was so impressed, they approved the idea.

56 ACT AS A COMPUTER CONSULTANT.

There's a big need for this type of help, and there are a couple ways to do it. Consider being a computer buddy. When a problem comes up, you are available to get calls for help. This is a great idea for

If You're A
9–10 Grade Parent

Participate in a public speaking program. **54**

Act as a computer consultant. **56**

Tutor one on one. **59**

Go to games and concerts. **41**

Vote for your school board members. **69**

parents who are particularly technologically proficient and who can receive calls at work.

If you can spare more time and you are free to go into the school, you can do something like what Barbara Ven Deventer accomplished. Three years ago, when her son was in fifth grade, she was speaking with her son's teacher at Mount View Elementary School in Unity, Maine. The teacher mentioned that although the school owned a computer software program designed to familiarize elementary-aged kids with the keyboard and with typing, nobody knew how to use it. Since Ven Deventer knew something about computers, she asked whether she could try to figure it out.

It took only two hours for her to acquaint herself with the program, which is called PAWS. Once she had familiarized herself with it, she wrote a booklet with clear, basic instructions—turn on the computer, turn on the monitor, insert the disk, and so on—so that other parent volunteers could come in and guide a group of kids through the lessons. She enlisted the help of four parents, and after a ten-minute introductory session, she and the parents would each come in for a half hour twice a week to work with the students on the school's seven computers. She made up progress sheets for the students so that it didn't matter whether or not a child worked on the same computer each week. Students could pick up where they had left off because the program could start at any level.

Ven Deventer also offered rewards for showing effort and progress, more than performance. Even the rewards, however, were computer-related: a coupon entitling the student to spend one session playing Carmen Sandiego or another computer game, in addition to working on the PAWS program.

As Ven Deventer came up with new lesson ideas, she would approach the school's volunteer coordinator, who then spoke to teachers and helped work out the logistics. Recently she took the entire sixth grade to the junior high school, where the computer room is big enough to accommodate them all. There she taught an introduction to Windows and word processing. Using just her own basic knowledge of computers, she developed a worksheet covering how to get into Windows, how to use a mouse, how to use word processing programs, how to save to a disk, and so on. She monitored their word-processing progress with a checklist that made sure they could change fonts, italicize, bold, or underline text, and make other formatting changes.

She also taught a number of students the basics of the Internet and the Web. Parents and students had to sign agreements that laid out how to behave responsibly on the Internet. During the sessions, Ven Deventer took the kids to the Yahoo site, because that seemed the most accessible, and instructed them to choose a subject to research and print out what they found so she could see they were successful.

57 START A SAFE-HOME CAMPAIGN.

Studies have shown that the more parents of teens confer about curfews, alcohol use, and chaperones, the more they are able to protect their children.

Presenting a united front, instead of feeling as if you are the only parent in town setting limits, is very effective. Of course, you can do this informally. But if you put it in writing, it sends an even stronger message to your kids. One great way to accomplish this is to establish a database of parents who have pledged that no parties will occur in their home without a chaperone and that no liquor will be available for minors.

58 HOLD A SAFE GRADUATION NIGHT.

This national group, with its roots in southern California, offers safe and sober all-night celebrations to keep kids off the streets on their graduation nights. Sandy DeGuire was motivated by several local tragedies to initiate a grad night at her children's high school in Lincoln, California. She first approached the PTA for the money to get started (about $500 to join the Grads Organization [see page 190] and get insurance, and $125 in fees for workshops offered by this member organization). Once she had the backing of the PTA she approached the principal of the high school and the superintendent to make sure she had the district's approval as well.

A typical grad night offers lots of entertainment—music, games, and prizes—and food to entice kids to stay at the party. Some schools do this on a small budget, offering only a band and food, but DeGuire had her sights set a little higher. Her goal was to raise $20,000 from the community. Her other goal was to have at least 200 of the 500 graduating students attend. (In the past, the high school had offered a program that bussed kids back and forth to a dancing cruise the night of their graduation, and that usually only had 75 to 100 participants.) In fact it was the latter goal that DeGuire was more concerned about achieving. She knew it would be a hard sell to convince these graduating seniors to want to be in a supervised environment on their big night.

The first step was to get organized. DeGuire began by sending out a flyer publicizing an informational meeting to let people know what she was doing. Sixty-five parents of seniors showed up. She gathered a core group of volunteers from this meeting, and they created letterhead for sending out solicitation letters. They knew it would be advantageous to name prominent backers on their letterhead so they requested endorsements from the mayor, the chief of police, the fire chief, and the local councilman. Then they sent letters appealing for funds to local businesses and to parents. (See pages 123–124 for sample letters; for additional material on which to model your own event, see 233–235 in the Appendix.)

Next, DeGuire started working towards her other goal—getting the students interested. She discovered every senior took history, and arranged to take some time out of that class to talk to the kids about grad night. The coordinator's opening comment at these talks was, "Graduation night can be the most dangerous night of your life." He then backed that statement up with statistics. After the serious part, volunteers showed students videos of other schools' grad nights, and sent around a survey asking what the kids would like at their grad night, so they would have a hand in planning it.

Meanwhile, DeGuire was looking for incentives. Besides providing tons of fun activities—a casino area, a jousting ring, a hypnotist, a make-your-own-video booth—she was gathering prizes to give away throughout the evening. As she was pricing different entertainment packages she asked businesses in the area to sponsor them. For example, one business sponsored the casino activity, while another supplied gift certificates to give away. One wealthy father donated a car as the grand prize, to be awarded at 5 a.m., only to someone who had stayed the whole night (students were allowed to leave, but could not return).

Tickets were sold from mid-February through graduation day, though the price got higher in monthly increments as an incentive for kids to buy early (prices ranged from $25 to $35). And there was work for volunteers to do on a daily, weekly, or drop-in basis. DeGuire herself ended up spending forty to fifty hours a week on the project, though it would have been less had she started sooner.

Despite the fact that the project didn't get started until February, in those three months, DeGuire gathered 120 volunteers, of which only half had senior children—some didn't have children in high school at all. She raised over $25,000, more than the goal. Even better, 325 students attended the party.

It was a huge success. It was held outside on a field behind the district offices, with access to a few indoor spaces with food and movies. The theme of the night was a time-warp, which graduates entered through a funky passageway filled with fog and bubbles. There were various big events, including bungee races; sumo wrestling, which took place in an inflatable ring with inflatable suits so competitors bounced off each other; and a jousting ring. There was a dance floor and an indoor cafe, one of seven locations for food.

Sample Grad Night Letter #1
to Parents and Community

Lincoln High School '97
Grad Night

High school graduation is a time to reflect on the past and look to the future. Many communities are faced with tragic losses on graduation night. Before our young grads ever have the chance to begin the next chapter of their future, they are faced with potentially the most dangerous night of their lives.

To keep our graduates safe this year, Lincoln High School is offering a Grad Night party for all graduates in the Lincoln District. A committee of parents and staff have been working since October to give our students an unforgettable evening of fun, excitement, exhilaration, and quiet moments. It will be a time for renewing old friendships and a time for good-byes. We are planning many types of activities for the evening such as casino games, carnival games, karaoke, DJ, videos, magicians, beach volleyball, and many, many more. We will also be providing food and beverages for the evening and prizes (stereos, TVs, radios, camera, cash, and so on), which all add to the excitement of the event.

The all-night grad party will take place at McCandless School, on graduation night, June 5,

1997, 10 p.m. until 5 a.m. The party is open to those students who will graduate in June from one of the schools in the Lincoln District.

There is still time for you to be part of planning this spectacular event. The construction and decorations committee is meeting at Brookside Farms every Tuesday evening, from 6 p.m. until 9:30 p.m. Help is greatly needed! There will be something for everyone to do. We are also looking for donations of prizes or cash to purchase prizes with. Having a large number of prizes is part of making a party like this a success.

If you have questions about Grad Night please contact Sandy DeGuire at 123-4567.

The only minor problem the whole evening involved noise complaints from neighboring houses. Though they thought they had planned for that sufficiently (especially since there was a police lieutenant volunteer), they still had to tone it down at one point during the night. They had anticipated having some intoxicated students and were planning to let them stay to keep them off the streets. It turned out that everyone was very well behaved.

For DeGuire, the evening's topper was a student's comment: "Mrs. DeGuire, when you said this would be fun, I didn't realize it would be this fun!"

59 TUTOR ONE ON ONE.

Meredith Coffin didn't have to think twice about volunteering when her kids entered elementary school in Unity, Maine. Her son had attended an alternative, parent-run nursery school and kindergarten where she got over the feeling that would have kept her out of the classroom—*What do I know about teaching?*

She continued to be involved all through elementary school in various ways, from just being present to help the teacher in the classroom, to bringing in a typing tutor for the sixth grade students. As her son approached junior high, how she could remain involved became an open-ended question.

A very good athlete was about to be kicked off her son's football team because of failing grades. Coffin was upset. She felt the school was not being supportive enough of this child's learning style. She shared her feelings with the guidance counselor, who suggested Coffin might privately tutor the student. When the counselor asked the boy, he agreed. Since Coffin is self-employed she was able to rearrange her schedule, and they started meeting for an hour-and-a-half once or twice a week during the last period of the school day, when most kids who weren't taking music or art had a free period. At the beginning they focused on the subject he was failing, but soon found he was doing better in that class but worse in the others. So they started going over all of his classwork together with the student reading the questions out loud, paraphrasing them (to be sure he understood), thinking them through, and so on. She broadened his studies with current events articles; they read them together, then discussed how they might be relevant to his school work and to his life in general.

Although Coffin didn't have any experience as a tutor, she knew it was important to get the child excited about learning and involve him in the learning process. And he did start doing better. Coffin feels what helped him was less the focus on specific studies than the verbal interaction and intellectual validation that came of having an adult focus on him for an extended period.

The real surprise for Coffin was when the boy's twin brother, an academic star, came in to the guidance office the following year to request a tutor. He figured if Coffin tutored him, he'd be able to really excel.

If You're An
11–12 Grade Parent

Be a career consultant. **65**

Start a high school alumni organization. **84**

Arrange internships for students in the
community. **87**

Hold a safe graduation night. **58**

Help out in the school library. **47**

60 WORK IN THE SCHOOL OFFICE.

Take it from me. The main office of a school is the
hub, the information center, the middle of the
educational universe. If you want to be where the
action is, and get a real inside view into how your
child's school works and the personalities at play,
volunteer in the office.

When her oldest daughter entered public school
in Wayne County, Michigan, Rhonda Collier
started volunteering in the school office, hoping
she would learn more about the school system.
Using skills from her former job as a secretary, she

walked into the school office and announced that whenever anyone needed anything typed up, copied, mailed, or other administrative tasks done, she would be glad to help. The staff began giving her things to do, and before she knew it, the PTA requested her secretarial services.

She is now the PTA secretary and takes notes at the meetings, makes and distributes flyers, and provides general support for parents and teachers. This kind of work gives her an insight into the public school system she feels she couldn't obtain any other way. For example, there is currently a bond issue coming up which she is working to help pass. Until now she didn't know what a bond was—she heard about it on the news but it didn't mean anything to her. Now she knows how important it is for the school: It will help funding and allow them to update computer labs to the level of all the surrounding school districts. Those districts are currently much better equipped because they have higher per-student budgets.

61 USE YOUR SECOND LANGUAGE.

If you are fluent in a second language, you can use

your knowledge to help out in the schools in lots of ways. To name a few:

- Offer teaching assistance in foreign language classes at school.
- Teach your own classes (if it's a language that's not already offered or if the school is understaffed).
- Teach English as a second language (ESL) for foreign students.
- Teach ESL for parents who may have trouble communicating with teachers or even with their kids.
- Organize a recreation workshop for kids to teach them some conversational phrases in a foreign language.
- Offer to teach an after-school class.
- Tutor kids who are studying that language.
- Donate books or movies in that language.
- If you are from a country where that language is spoken, volunteer to come in as a guest speaker.

62 BE A MYSTERY READER.

Research suggests that reading to children often

improves literacy. So as a guest reader or a book pal you can really help less fortunate children in the school. It can also be a way of sharing books you and your child love with a larger group. Your reading can be part of your child's class, an early-morning treat for kids dropped off before school starts, or part of an indoor recess program in cold weather. To jazz it up, you could arrange for a whole day of readers to come, costumed as book characters. I don't know of a teacher who wouldn't be happy to have a parent provide this activity. There's no extra work involved, no cost to the teacher, except maybe offering an idea of a relevant book. There also is no ques-

IF YOU'RE A
SINGLE PARENT

Invite your child's teacher home. **2**

Provide transportation. **70**

Start a school support program at your place of work. **76**

Don't miss your school's open house night. **27**

Make the most of your parent-teacher conferences. **40**

tion that a child would feel proud to see his parent in a reading role.

63 PUT ON A TALENT SHOW.

While many schools have long produced student plays, few seem to think of putting on a more generalized song and dance event. A talent show works especially well for younger students who may not be ready for the commitment of rehearsals and memorizing lines. Plus, it levels the playing field, so to speak, by including all sorts of different skills.

Cane Run Elementary School in Louisville, Kentucky, has been holding a talent show for a few years. Initiated by a conversation between the principal, arts instructors, and a couple of parents, the show is now run by Lisa Fennison, who also serves as PTA president. There is always a lot of student interest—this year forty acts signed up to audition: fourteen dancing acts, nineteen singing, two magic, two miscellaneous (a wrestling re-enactment and a comedy act), and three class-wide acts. PTA and faculty members audition and choose each act on the basis of skill and level of difficulty, though there's always a mix of ages (the school is K–5). All the participants get a certificate and medal.

There is a nighttime performance open to the public and a daytime performance for the student body. Fennison advertises the show on local cable channels and has it announced on the community bulletin board at the local cable access station. The show takes practically no money to put together (unless they opt to have a refreshment stand). For the past few years they've been charging $1 admission per adult and have been using the profits to refurbish the stage. Last year they bought new curtains, an investment of over $1,000, and this year they plan to buy new lighting and sound equipment.

64 HELP TEAM TEACHING GET A FOOTHOLD.

Meredith Coffin, of Unity, Maine, was involved in advocating a new team-teaching program in her high school's ninth grade. The idea is that core teachers—one from science, one from language arts, and one from history—work together to teach a class of students all focusing on the same unit or topic but from different perspectives. So, during a unit on shipwrecks, the language arts instructor would have the students write a short story about what it would be like to be in a shipwreck, or read a book where there was a shipwreck; the history teacher might focus on the economic conditions that have led to shipwrecks in the past; the science teacher might talk about weather systems, or the physics of what brings a ship under water.

Four ninth grade teachers got a grant to develop this new program and invited Coffin and another parent to help evaluate it and explain it to other teachers and parents. They took a trip to a school in southern Maine where they attended some team-teaching seminars and classes, then pooled their thoughts and responses before presenting them to anyone else. Coffin says having the mix of parents and teachers was helpful because while teachers noticed things like how the block scheduling worked and other logistical concerns teachers taking on this program would have to figure out, parents saw it from their child's point of view, noting what a good model it would be for kids to see their teachers working and problem solving together.

The group of parents and teachers presented the team-teaching idea to the entire high school faculty and then to the school board; all were in favor of the new program. It is now set to begin next year.

65 BE A CAREER CONSULTANT.

If you have a career, sharing how you prepared for it, what your workday is like, and what you like about your work is a wonderful way to help introduce students to the "real" world.

Mary Ann Tina had three boys in the Ardsley, New York, schools when she decided she wanted to get more involved in their education. So she took what was then a small, part-time position in the Youth Employment Office in Ardsley High School. Back then, the office's main function was to help kids find part-time and summer jobs.

But as businesses started to require more of the youths they hired, she began helping students think about career direction, write resumes, and talk about what the work world is really like.

Now the main goal of the office is to "bridge the world of school with the outside world." Besides helping students find part-time and summer jobs, Tina helps coordinate externships, work-study projects, and the Capstone program; all offer school credit. For an externship, Tina helps the student determine what kind of environment he would like to work in, and then draws on her network of parents, community members, and local businesses to find a place where the student can volunteer in his chosen field. The student volunteers sixty hours outside of school over the course of a year and gains one-quarter credit toward his diploma—and some work experience. According to Tina, there are about forty or fifty students who participate in this program each year.

The work-study program allows students to leave school in the afternoon to work at a part-time job (for pay). These students receive one full credit for 300 hours of work. The Capstone program involves work-placement arrangements for special-needs students.

Along with these employment services, Tina's office serves as an information resource for career trends and advice. She reads the newspapers and government publications, and requests that organizations and businesses donate free materials about employment and career development.

Tina advises any parent wishing to career counsel students to "use [their] community as a resource." She says almost every community has a storehouse of knowledge and experience kids can draw on. One easy way to connect kids with the community is to pull together panels of people in different occupations and bring them in to talk to the kids.

For example, Tina went to the hospital in a neighboring community and signed up a physical therapist, an x-ray technician, a nurse, and a doctor to represent the medical profession, while she found several parents who are lawyers to come in and talk about their work. Tina has also done this with the local newspaper, and she suggests that one may even want to bring together several school employees—teacher, guidance counselor, principal, librarian—to give kids an idea of what their high school is like behind the scenes. Kids who are interested in a profession may follow up with a shadow experience, spending a day following someone in her occupation and getting exposure to the workplace.

66 TEACH A DRAMA CLASS.

Drama skills are life skills, and all children can benefit from learning them. When my older son was in third grade at a Brooklyn school, I was on sabbatical. I mentioned to his teacher that I'd taught drama, and that I would love to come in and do a drama class with the kids. I held eight sessions with the whole class in the classroom. We pushed aside desks and did exercises using the imagination. We played concentration games, made up characters, moved around the room as if it had peanut butter on the floor, pretended we were chewing gum and guessed whether or not it was real. *Improvisation* by Viola Spolin or *Drama in the Classroom* by Nellie McCaslin are good reference books. They have blueprints for exercises and even provide comments you can use for coaching. Throughout the class, I tried to let the children know that it is safe to take risks, at least when it comes to drama.

We didn't end with a performance, although you can if you have the time. The course tied in to the curriculum because we used vocabulary words from their spelling lists. The teacher appreciated my contribution. It was so worthwhile for me, my son, and the whole class. An unexpected result: The teacher felt comfortable enough to do it herself the following year.

67 EXPLORE A VIDEO MONITORING SYSTEM.

This is one of the more futuristic ideas in the book. I don't think anyone has tried it yet in a regular school setting, but more than twenty child-care centers around the country have been wired to let parents watch their children via an Internet service. Although the systems on the market are in various stages of development, the general way they work so far is with closed-circuit television cameras in the child-care center. The camera sends video images to a Web site that can only be accessed by parents using a special password.

There are a lot of concerns this kind of monitoring raises, from expense to a certain kind of "Big Brother" mentality. But I think it's worth more research and experimentation to see how we can make it work for the good of the children, parents, and teachers. Imagine the possibilities if such a system were in place at your child's school. You could check out whether your child is daydreaming in class or actively engaged. You could observe a teacher's style firsthand but without making the teacher self-conscious. You could find out how your child is interacting with other kids.

IF YOU HAVE MORE THAN ONE CHILD

Write a letter to your child's school principal in the spring. **15**

Decorate! **30**

Start an after-school club. **34**

Become a community communicator. **88**

Run for the school board. **73**

If you are intrigued and want more information, companies providing this service are listed in chapter five on pages 202 and 203.

68 BECOME A PARENT LIAISON.

Sometimes it takes a parent to help another parent get involved. Olga Ferrer, of Cleveland, Ohio, is one of twenty-five parent volunteers in Buhrer Elementary School every day. Sometimes she helps out in the classroom, but usually she works in the office, helping with administrative tasks and helping parents who have problems. She feels the most important thing she can do as a volunteer is to welcome other parents and volunteers to be involved and feel comfortable in the schools. Because she herself is so comfortable with the school administration, she is an ideal link between the two worlds.

CHAPTER FOUR

COMMUNITY PARTNERS

Twenty-two things parents can do outside the school or home.

Think of this chapter as a Chinese restaurant menu, not a smorgasbord. If you pick even one or two things to do, that is terrific.

69 VOTE FOR YOUR SCHOOL BOARD MEMBERS.

If I said you could help pick the next principal, wouldn't you want to be involved in such an important decision? Think about it: By voting for the school board members of your choice, you are indirectly guiding the hiring throughout the district. Yet voter turnout for school board elections is notoriously low. Parents who think of themselves as very involved still end up skipping this key step. Voting is such a simple and quick way to make your voice heard and make a difference in the education of your child—and all the children in your district.

Of course, it doesn't mean much unless your vote is an informed decision. It's part of the voter's responsibility to find out what each candidate's views are on a variety of subjects. How? If there is a local newspaper, chances are it will run a special issue with the candidates' printed statements. Many districts hold sessions for the public to meet and question candidates. If you have a friend who is knowledgeable about school affairs and whose judgment you trust implicitly, go ahead and ask his advice.

It's easy to vote a lazy ballot. By that I mean voting for someone because you happen to know the person from the neighborhood or a sports team or because they seem attractive or have a good sense of humor. Instead, these are the kinds of questions I'd like parents to consider before voting:

- What is the candidate's specific educational philosophy? Does she favor core curriculum or child-centered learning? Experimental math or teaching by the book? Traditional or progressive?

- Is the candidate obsessed with any single issue (firing a principal, slashing the budget, or building a new tennis court)?

- Does the candidate seem sincerely interested in and committed to the education of all the district's children?

- How would this candidate rate issues that are important to you? If you want athletics de-emphasized and the arts beefed up, does this candidate rank art ahead of the football team when it comes to budgets? How about teachers' pay, computer technology, or gifted programs?

- Where does this candidate stand on any proposed budget?

- Does this candidate have a background that would make her a good school board member?

70 PROVIDE TRANSPORTATION.

Often there are others who would like to volunteer but don't have transportation. You could shuttle senior citizens back and forth to schools or libraries to help in tutoring programs. Or you could drive neighbors to vote on school district budgets or to school board meetings. It might seem like a small way to be involved, but it's these little things that often make the difference between a budget passing or not.

You can informally offer a lift to people whenever you're going their educational way. You also could organize a more formal way of letting others know you're available to drive on a regular basis:

- Put an announcement in the local newspaper.
- Post flyers in stores and other public places.
- Tell your school's principal and school board members to spread the word.
- Let the staff at local retirement homes know.
- List yourself in a skills directory (see page 172).

71 FORM AN ELECTION COMMITTEE.

This is a temporary commitment. It involves working to encourage voter turnout around election times. You can do it by telephone, by printing up flyers, by giving informal informational talks, or by holding debates between candidates. A committee is especially useful when complicated issues, such as the school budget, are on the ballot. The committee can help educate the public before people vote.

72 ATTEND SCHOOL BOARD MEETINGS.

So many parents I speak with really do not have a clear understanding of the role that a school board plays in their children's education.

The school board of education is usually made up of between three and fourteen residents elected to represent the community in decisions about the schools. The group meets once or twice a month to discuss issues that come up in the district, as well as budget and personnel issues (though these will sometimes be brought up in private sessions). There is time allotted at each meeting for residents and parents to speak to the board, and agendas and minutes of previous meetings should be available at libraries and the district clerk's office.

A lot of important decision making goes on at these meetings: how the school budget is allotted, how teachers are evaluated, how and why curriculum decisions are made. Whether you want to give your two cents on an issue and try to make a difference or listen and stay abreast of what's going on in your district, attending the school board meeting regularly is an important way to stay involved.

If there is something you want to change or some new program you want to enact, it's good to gather support from the community before approaching the board. You may want to talk to other parents or even send around a petition before you raise your suggestion at a meeting. Agendas are set by the school board president and superintendent, but if there are issues you want to see discussed, try a school-based management committee, or your principal. Otherwise go to a board meeting and raise the issue during comments and questions.

For example, you could raise your hand and say, *I've always been interested in chess clubs. I'd like to ask who I should talk to.* Or you could call a board member before the meeting.

When you're at a meeting, don't hesitate to raise questions as they occur to you. Try to be as brief as possible. This is not the appropriate forum for speeches or diatribes. It's important to be polite and open minded when you phrase your questions and/or your comments. You're unlikely to get results if you're hostile. Instead of saying, *I think it's outrageous that the school board has made this stupid decision. Don't you people know how dangerous it is out there? I will not have my child standing in the middle of the street,* try a more circumspect approach such as, *I know the school board has voted to cut down the number of school bus stops, but I don't understand why. Could you please explain the reasoning for us?*

Another example: You could say something like, *I think it's ridiculous that you're spending so much on athletics. How dare you raise the football team budget by twenty percent when we should be spending that money on books?* Such a comment practically requires the school board to become defensive instead of clarifying the situation. Whereas if you asked a question: *Is there a reason why the budget for the football team has gone up so much this year?* you might get the following response: *Yes, there is; we had to have a second team because so many more kids are going out for football, plus we had to hire another coach.* You might still disagree with the board's decision, but at least you'll have a more satisfying response.

Pay attention to how board members respond to people: Do they seem to be listening and giving satisfying responses or offering to find out more information? Even a board member doesn't have all the answers, but what you're looking for is the kind of person who will say, *There's still a lot I don't know, but I'll find out for you.*

73 RUN FOR THE SCHOOL BOARD.

Short of becoming a teacher or home schooling, this is probably the most involved a parent can be in education.

Penny Delany, mother of four, first ran for school board in 1990 and has been on it since, except for one year. She served as president of the board for three terms. Her involvement is all the more impressive in light of the fact that three out of her four children attend schools outside the district she serves. This is what she has to say about her experience:

If you're thinking of running for school board, your very first step is to attend school board meetings and see what the school board does. It's not necessary to go for years and years. I went for several months to see what the job really looks like. Does what they do fit with your personal strengths? For example, you might not like public speaking, which a school board member has to do regularly. (Not only that, but as a public figure, when you speak you have to be very careful and realize you will be quoted.)

Make sure you understand what the role of the school board is and identify and familiarize yourself with the local issues, even if you don't understand all the pros and cons. Then you can decide if it would be more satisfying to be a parent involved in a committee.

School board members are policy makers, not administrators. Your role is to communicate with voters and serve as an advocate for the school system. If you expect to get involved in the nitty-gritty of running your child's school, you're going to be disappointed. You spend relatively little time on curriculum issues. It's unlikely you'll get your hands dirty. What's more likely is that you will have access to information on curriculum when there are any disputes or reviews of curriculum. Even then, you might have a fairly superficial involvement with the curriculum. Sometimes that can be frustrating. It's usually not conducive to in-depth discussions.

You do get to make big decisions that ultimately can affect little decisions: The board votes on who will be the superintendent, same with principals and teacher appointments. But we don't actually interview candidates. We are a lot more involved with administrative positions. We just hired the director of special education, for example.

You definitely receive a lot of information other parents might not get. One reason is that individual parents will call you with very specific stories and questions. I do tell parents to start from the bottom up when they have a problem. So you'd go first to the teacher, then the principal, then the superintendent, and only last to the school board. Sometimes, though, a parent wants the board to know about a situation or complaint on an informal basis. In one case of a student suspension, the parent was quite upset and requested a private meeting with the board. We listened to her in a sort of hand-holding capacity.

Although it does take a lot of time, you can run for school board if you work. In fact, more often than not, board members are full-time working parents. I would say I put in twenty-five to thirty hours a week. The minimum time commitment for meetings alone is eight hours a month, with maybe ten hours a month for reading the board packets the superintendent generates once a week. Also you spend a lot of time having phone conversations.

You are involved—more than most people probably want to be—in the budget process. That takes a lot of your energy and time, along with many other financial and legal issues: running things behind the scenes, legal issues with unions, grievances, board reviews, and contract negotiations.

Once you are elected, try not to take things personally. Always try to keep your temper. You're in a public position: If you lose your temper, then you lose support. I was sort of a moderate among some extreme groups. I was able to understand both sides. It was satisfying to be a voice of reason.

74 WRITE A GRANT PROPOSAL.

This a good idea for a parent who has little time available during the school day. Unlike direct fund raising, researching and writing a grant proposal offers more flexible hours.

A grant lets parents in Atlanta call the Homework Hotline, an interactive electronic mailbox service accessed via telephone. We had this system at P.S. 75, too, as I mentioned in the introduction. Teachers leave daily messages for parents with one- to three-minute descriptions about that day in school and that night's homework. Parents may also hear messages from the principal, PTA, and other school personnel. Think of other things your school could use to help you stay involved, and propose writing grants to obtain them.

When writing a grant, you need to keep in mind the following general points:

- Be as specific as possible in describing your project or service.

- Describe why the school or school district needs it. What problem would be solved?

- Try to use as many statistics and other facts as you can muster.

- Describe how the project would address the problem.

- Outline how the success of the program would be evaluated.

- Provide a detailed budget.

- Explain how the program would be able to continue when the grant money ran out: Would it count on other sources, be self-supporting, or have a self-limiting time period?

75 SERVE ON A SCHOOL ADVISORY COMMITTEE.

These might be called site committees, compact for learning, support team, or any number of other names. Membership is comprised of parents, teachers, administration, community, or sometimes even children. As the name implies, these committees are meant to advise, to suggest and review policy,

---

If You Want to Write a Grant

There are entire books on the subject of grant writing and grant requirements. Begin at your public library with the *Foundation Directory* and *Corporate Giving Directory.*

Once you've narrowed down likely places to submit your grant, refer to one or more of the following titles for in-depth help:

The Complete Guide to Getting a Grant, by Laurie Blum.

Grant Writing for Teachers, by Linda Karges-Bone.

Grants for Nonprofit Organizations, by Eleanor Gilpatrick.

Grant Writing Basics, by Jessica Morrell.

but not to vote directly on staffing, curriculum, or other issues.

Deborah Farr, mother of two, teaches substance abuse classes (part of the state's required health education curriculum) at Marlborough Elementary School in Marlborough, Connecticut. While at that job several years ago, she discovered the district's Instructional Support Team. She approached her children's elementary school principal with the idea of starting a similar group. He was less than enthusiastic at first, but as Farr talked to more people, interest grew. She found the idea was becoming more common and other schools in the area were taking action, so eventually the principal conceded.

The School Advisory Council (SAC) Deborah Farr is now involved with has representation from every part of the community—school support staff, administration and faculty, parents representing the different student age groups, and community members who don't have kids (to add a perspective that might otherwise have been ignored).

The group meets once a month directly after school. This meeting time has caused some dissent from parents who would like to serve on the council but can't because they are working, but the time has not yet been changed for fear that teachers would not make the trip home and back if it were moved to the evening.

According to Farr, SAC acts as a right arm to the administration and staff. They cannot make decisions about policies or procedures as the board of education does, but when issues come up among parents or faculty, they often are brought to the SAC first. For example, Farr's group began a task force on homework, studying how much, how often, and why it's given, with the aim of generating a plan or consensus. After the group considers an issue, the faculty decide where to go with it. Other issues they've dealt with include the role of holiday celebrations in the school, which came up because some parents were concerned about separation of church and state and the students' different religions, and field trips—how many there should be, what they should involve, what their purpose is.

Most of SAC's discussions come from a letter or phone call from a concerned parent. The results of each meeting are published in the school newsletter and distributed to the community.

76 START A SCHOOL SUPPORT PROGRAM AT YOUR PLACE OF WORK.

When Eric Hochberg of Altadena, California, worked for the Xerox Company, part of his official work week included tutoring some fifth grade students in science as part of a company-sponsored program. That was five years ago. Today, more and more businesses, from large national corporations to small mom-and-pop companies, are getting involved in education.

IBM provided schools in Charlotte, North Carolina, with software called Wired for Learning. It lets parents and teachers contact each other, but also parents can use the software to receive homework assignments, see their children's completed work, and find teacher evaluations. If a family doesn't have an online service or a computer, they can use the school's computer labs, which are open evenings and weekends. They can also use the service at a community center located in the public housing project where many of the district's children live. In exchange for using the software, IBM asks parents to sign a contract agreeing to volunteer at the school an hour each week for each of their children. They can help out in the classroom, tutor kids, or work on special events. More than 200 parents have signed the contract and been trained to use the software in the few months it's been available.

Representatives from a project called PIECES (Parents, Industry, Educators Cooperating for Education Success) in Newton, North Carolina, went to a local hosiery manufacturer to ask if guidance counselors could meet parents at the work site. The company, Ridgeview, Inc., has 325 employees. Now counselors visit the work site once a month and meet with each parent for fifteen minutes, and the employees still receive pay for that time. Counselors bring students' records, report cards, and comments from teachers. The program has been especially good at reaching noncustodial fathers, who had little prior contact with the schools. Ridgeview has become increasingly supportive of this program, and now offers employees with the company for more than five years extra paid vacation days so they can volunteer for school field trips or other school activities.

Before approaching your employer about participating in a school district program, be sure to do your homework. Have ready a list of the advantages to the school *and* the business. A business, for example, could benefit from:

- An opportunity to gain positive publicity.
- Receiving tax deductions.
- Helping create a future pool of better-educated employees.
- Fostering good will.

The U.S. Department of Education offers ready-made materials that you can order for your employer.

The agency's Partnership for Family Involvement in Education's "Employers for Learning" program is free. It includes a brief application for the company to fill out and an "Employers for Learning Promise" certificate. The "promise" is that an employer will recognize there are many ways to get involved:

- Contact a local school to discuss opportunities for cooperation.

- Explore with employees ways they can help children learn.

- Explore with employees ways they can help local schools better educate their students.

- Explore company policy and practices to encourage and enable employee involvement in schools and learning.

- Get more information from the Partnership for Family Involvement in Education.

Next the employer makes this commitment:

- Identify a contact person authorized to explore and develop options for company involvement in our family/school/community initiatives.

- Take action to implement programs.

- Share best practices after evaluating programs annually.

- Form partnerships with other stakeholders to promote, implement, and improve family-friendly policies and practices.

For information on getting *your* employer on board, write to the Partnership for Family Involvement in Education (see page 201).

77 START A SCHOOL-COMMUNITY PARTNERSHIP.

In almost every community there are institutions or organizations that could help the schools and provide unique opportunities for students and teachers. This kind of collaboration is mutually beneficial, whether it's senior citizens gaining the company of children or an institution gaining the respect and loyalty of the community. Here are a few places you might consider beginning such a partnership:

- Churches.
- Synagogues.
- Community centers.
- Hospitals.
- Labor unions or American Legion organizations.
- Libraries.

- Local businesses.
- Colleges and universities.
- Other schools.
- Cultural institutions.
- Social service organizations.
- Senior citizen organizations.

All of these places can be valuable sources of information, volunteers, space, or other helpful materials. For example, social service organizations or cultural institutions could provide educational workshops for kids in their areas of expertise while churches, synagogues, and other community centers can offer volunteer help for tutoring or mentoring programs out of or in the schools. Senior citizens can introduce crocheting, knitting, quilting, and embroidery to students who don't have an extended family.

The Jefferson County Public School District in Louisville, Kentucky, has formed partnerships with, among many others, Humana, Inc., a national health service provider; the Boy Scouts of America; and the Kentuckiana Education and Workforce Institute.

In New Haven, Connecticut, the Hospital of Saint Raphael, a nonprofit healthcare institution with about 3,000 employees, decided to create an after-school reading room for local families. The neighborhood didn't have a public library. The reading room is in space the New Haven Police Department provided for free and is staffed by volunteers from the hospital. Hospital employees and the hospital's auxiliary donate books to the reading room, which is also stocked with reference materials, maps, and computers. Volunteers also help children with homework and communicate with parents on their child's progress.

The Chicago Children's Museum has a partnership with the Robert Taylor Community Schools. Called Taylor Action, it funds programs to foster parent volunteerism and leadership in the schools and community. The goal of the program, begun in 1992 and now with several different branches, is to empower parents to take more control over their schools and community life.

Robin Williams, a mother of three and a Robert Taylor Community resident, first got involved with the Museum's "Books Alive" Program when the teacher she was already working with asked for some extra help. A facilitator from the museum and parent volunteers traveled from location to location in the community with different books each week, held a discussion group, and led trips and activities related to the book—all sponsored by the museum.

IF YOU'RE A
STAY-AT-HOME PARENT

Start a school newspaper or literary magazine. **35**
Work in the school office. **60**
Start a local education foundation. **81**
Run a nature program. **33**
Use your second language. **61**

Since then she's held various positions with the Taylor Action Program, ranging from treasurer to program coordinator. Her sons are now ten, eleven, and thirteen, and she's been volunteering in the schools for over six years. She believes strongly in the program's "each one teach one" philosophy: Each parent who gains new leadership or career skills should teach them to one other person in the community. Through this passing-it-on the community and the schools empower themselves—the best kind of partnership.

The Partnership for Family Involvement in Education can help through its "Community Organizations for Learning" program (see page 201).

78 RUN CLASSES FOR PARENTS.

Classes for parents can be the cornerstone of a parental involvement campaign. Subjects may range from communicating better with children, to helping them read, to sex education, to discipline issues. It might be a one-time class with a special focus or a more formal series given through a community college, a church, or the YMCA. It can be a parent-to-parent organization that hosts discussion groups. School guidance counselors often are willing to moderate these events, and provide a professional perspective.

A parent involvement program in Salem, Oregon, offers parenting classes with a focus on drug and alcohol abuse in families. In addition, a "Parents-Staff-Together" training program develops parental leadership through monthly meetings held in parent homes.

Olga Ferrer has been a parent facilitator for Buhrer Elementary's collaboration with Baldwin Wallace College. The college offers workshops and classes on parenting skills and parent-child communication called "Homework without Tears" for parents at this Cleveland public school. Ferrer sends out flyers and makes phone calls, advertising the classes and welcoming the parents to invite family members or friends.

Ferrer herself was certified to teach parenting classes through an eight-week course given by the

Cleveland Board of Education. The response to the parenting class has been great—last time she graduated sixty-two parents. She also teaches drug and alcohol and child abuse classes in the elementary and high schools through a group called Hispanic Umapos, a counseling agency. She just finished with a ten-week child-abuse prevention program in the elementary school.

79 START A PARENT CENTER.

One of the most ambitious and successful variations on parenting classes I've come across is in Natchez, Mississippi. There, the Natchez-Adams School District runs a Parent Center to help involve families who want to improve their children's academic achievement. The U.S. Department of Education describes how a Parent Center works in one of its publications:

The first step is a school/family conference. During the conference the teacher explains the area where the child is having difficulty and completes a Parent Assistance Form, known as the "green sheet." This form indicates the skill the teacher would like the student to work on in the next six-week period (e.g., long division). The parent then takes the green sheet to the Parent Center where staff provide materials to promote skills in the indicated area. They also demonstrate to the parent how to use the materials with her child at home. Materials might include games, manipulatives, and puzzles, and focus on activity-based learning. Parents can check out materials for as long as they wish to work with their child. After a parent has attended the center, a follow-up form is sent to the referring teacher informing them of the parent's visit. Parents can also attend year-round workshops through the Parent Center. Workshop topics range from discipline and building self-esteem to academic subjects. Whenever parents participate in a workshop or use the center's other services, the child's teacher is informed.

80 LINE UP EXPERTS IN A FIELD.

Once you pick an area of the school you feel could use the most outside help, approach those you know—or those you know who know someone— who have some expertise. Parents in a school in East Harlem were equal partners in running the performing arts curriculum. They scouted the best programs to motivate kids in the performing arts. At P. S. 75, we contacted Xerox to pay for some programs, but we also asked parents, "Who do you know who does something interesting, who can get involved with the school and set up tutoring programs, not just a one-shot deal, but on an ongoing basis?" They made a list and brought Raul Julia and Pete Seeger into the school. I could never have reached performers like them on my own.

81 START A LOCAL EDUCATION FOUNDATION.

There is no doubt in my mind that this is a huge movement. Right now, there are twenty-seven education foundations in Westchester County, New York, where I live and work, and the number is growing. As a direct response to the budget hit many districts have taken in the last decade, the mission of a foundation is to supplement or enhance a school district's curriculum. An education foundation takes up where a PTA leaves off: While a PTA tends to deal in small amounts of money for hands-on, parent-child activities, a foundation focuses on large amounts of private money for curriculum enrichment. A foundation is an independent incorporated entity without the structure—some would say constraints—of a PTA, which is part of a national organization. In most cases, the foundation and PTA can complement each other nicely.

In fact, Ronda Billig and Roberta Samberg of Irvington, New York, were asked to start an education foundation in 1996 by their PTA. Several PTA members had been studying the idea of education foundations and felt they were the wave of the future. They also agreed that there was a need. The town hadn't had a school play in five years. The elementary school had grown from 500 to 800 students almost overnight.

Billig and Samberg, both former lawyers, had been running the annual holiday happening, a big, successful community event. Billig says she felt that if she accepted the challenge of starting a foundation, she'd "never have to bake another cookie again." The first step was to pick an executive board as a steering committee. The PTA suggested some people, and Billig and Samberg found others with particular skills they needed represented on the board. The treasurer is a math professor at a local college, for instance. Billig says a foundation is a good vehicle for people with expertise to make a substantive contribution, to pick and choose interesting issues.

The next step was to find a lawyer who had already helped other local education foundations become incorporated. Billig says that was essential because the paperwork and bureaucratic requirements are otherwise daunting. They also put out the word that they needed a board of directors. They asked the superintendent, school board, and the PTA to sit *ex officio* on the board. Billig says this was a key move because they didn't want the board questioning what the foundation was up to, nor did they want to be in competition with the PTA.

For working/voting board members, they looked for people to represent every neighborhood, every ethnic group, men and women who were comfortable with money and/or generating money, artists—as much of a cross section as possible. After compiling a list of fifty potential members, they held an organizing dessert-and-coffee evening. Out of that gathering, a board almost "self-selected" itself.

With a solid board of directors, the group got together to write a position paper describing a foundation and why one was needed. Meanwhile, it became a legal, tax-exempt entity. An initial mailing raised $30,000. A gala raised $27,000, and now they're working on a Con Ed grant, as well as an annual report to list everybody who has donated money, from $25 to $5,000.

Sample Letter from a
Local Education Foundation

Richmond Education Foundation
Reaching for Excellence

Dear Neighbor:

We are writing to propose an opportunity for you to make a tremendous difference in the lives of young people in the Richmond community.

As you well know, these are challenging times in education and the need for private support for public education has never been greater. Shrinking tax bases, cutbacks in state aid, and expanded enrollments have put pressure on our educational system at a time when the demands for educating tomorrow's generation have never been greater.

Members of the Richmond community have joined together in a commitment to provide support to our schools through the establishment of the Richmond Education Foundation, a not-for-profit organization whose mission is to develop independent, voluntary sources of funding to support significant school projects and programs. We believe our children are worthy of your support, and we hope that you will join the growing number of parents, residents, and local businesses by contributing to the Foundation's efforts to enhance the education of every child in Richmond.

Here is an example of the difference your support can make. Thanks to the early gifts of several generous contributors this year, plans are already under way to restore the high school play and mount an original musical at the elementary school. In future years we hope to become a catalyst for innovative programs and fund grants in science, history, literature, technology, and athletics in all three schools.

We believe that Richmond stands second to none in its support for quality education, but that the strains and controversies of recent years indicate a need to find other ways to express that commitment. The challenges we face are not beyond the capacities of this community, but, to face them, we must act together. We have included some additional information on the Foundation, its goals, and mission. We believe the Richmond Education Foundation is worthy of your support and we ask you to join with your neighbors and give to it wholeheartedly.

Sincerely,
The Board of Directors

The foundation itself initiated the first program it sponsored: The PTA had come up with a couple of volunteers to teach art in six elementary school classes. But the school has thirty-seven classes. So the foundation hired a team of six artists who come into every classroom once a week. They are like artists-in-residence.

The rest of the funds were awarded by soliciting grants with applications submitted mostly by teachers. The foundation's grant committee presented ideas to the school board to keep them in the loop and to get their recommendations. Some grant requests—computers and VCRs—were rejected on the basis that they were the school board's responsibility. Out of eighteen projects the first year, eleven were funded, including the following:

- The "Jason" program, an interdisciplinary study of ocean environments and how they affect life on earth.

- "Art through the Ages," which integrates periods in art with their corresponding periods in social studies and English.

- A state-of-the-art printer for the publishing center at the elementary school.

- A high school play.

- An architectural design and drafting program (an

upgrade of an old-fashioned shop class) for grades 9–12.

- An urban-orienteering walk around historic New York for seventh graders.
- A Dutch-colonial program for fourth graders.
- A puppet show for kindergarten.
- A naturalist to make bird masks with second graders.

If being able to supplement your child's curriculum this way appeals to you, I suggest you start by contacting an already established local education foundation for information. In the very near future I'm sure there will be national organizations providing resources as well. Meanwhile, you can refer to pages 164–165 for more sample education foundation material.

82 CONDUCT A SURVEY.

Pinpoint a problem in your school or school district and devise a questionnaire to gather information. After you've tabulated the results, present your findings to the school board, the principal, the parents' organization, or other influential groups.

For example, I know of parents in one district who were concerned that the high cost of field trips was a burden on some families. They feared there were children who were missing out on some wonderful educational experiences because of lack of money. So they sent a questionnaire to all parents, asking for anonymous responses, of course. Armed with actual data on how many families felt pinched financially, they were able to get the school district to establish a fund to help these families pay for field trips.

83 HOST A FIELD TRIP AT YOUR WORKPLACE.

At first glance, you might think where you work is either unsuitable or uninteresting as a destination for students. But it's amazing how much a child can soak up from the most seemingly routine places. For younger grades, a visit to a construction site, pizzeria, or farm would be fun and educational. Invite older children to your office and give them a close-up look at whatever business you're in.

If this idea intrigues you, follow these steps:

- Approach either the principal or an individual teacher with your invitation.

- Discuss what size group you can accommodate.

- Decide what time of day would be best for all concerned.

- Think about the logistics of transporting children and help make it as easy as possible for the school.

- Make a plan for what exactly you will do once students are at your workplace. Will you give them a brief introductory talk and then a guided tour? Will there be activities for them to do? Discuss ahead of time with the teacher or teachers involved so they can prepare the children to gain the most educational benefit.

- Try to end the visit with some sort of treat: a special snack, a token piece of equipment or supply, or some other memorabilia.

84 START A HIGH SCHOOL ALUMNI ORGANIZATION.

If your school is old enough to have graduated a good number of students, this can be a terrific way to spread an even wider net to pull in resources. The idea is to have volunteers organize and run the alumni society, which could publish newsletters about the school and its graduates, hold reunions, and solicit donations. Alumni often respond gener-ously to very specific requests for help such as fix-ing a flood-damaged gym floor they remember fondly playing basketball on or establishing a "chair" to honor a beloved, exceptional teacher or bringing back the art program that led to a career in graphic design and has now been cut for bud-getary reasons.

An alumni organization is one of those efforts that takes time to pan out. It will build slowly as graduates are able to help the school through their own con-tacts with colleges, corporations, and other commu-nities. This networking can lead to gifts or loans of equipment, internships, career advice, dropout pre-vention programs, and all kinds of other aid.

A good first place to start is at your high school's reunions. Find out when and where they are held, contact the chairperson, and ask permission to make a short appeal on the spot.

85 SET UP A SATELLITE TOWN MEETING.

On the third Tuesday of each month during the school year, U.S. Secretary of Education Richard Riley hosts the Satellite Town Meeting, a cost-free, live, interactive TV program about community efforts to improve teaching and learning. You can ask the secretary and his various guest experts questions on what is working in other schools. If you want to participate, just follow these steps:

- Call 1-800-872-5327 to get registration forms, a schedule of topics, satellite coordinates, and help from information specialists on how to organize your local meeting.
- Arrange for a site with satellite capability.
- Bring together parents, teachers, businesspeople, and community leaders.
- Call your local cable operator to broadcast the program throughout your community.

Topics for the 1997-98 series included improving student achievement, using technology in classrooms, providing access to college, supporting high-quality teachers, creating safe schools, teaching algebra, and improving reading skills.

86 DEVELOP A SKILLS DIRECTORY.

You find volunteers throughout your community, list what they're available to do and what their qualifications are, and distribute a booklet to teachers and principals. Try to be as open and creative as possible when thinking about what people might offer. Do you know someone who can knit? Make music? Repair telephones? Fix toilets? Teach karate? Take photographs? Speak Japanese? Train computer programmers? Plant flowers? Provide child care at meetings?

If someone says, *But I don't have any skills,* show her a preliminary list of areas you are seeking listings for to jog her memory. It's amazing how many things people can do or know and how fast they forget they can do them or know them! For example, a nurse knows CPR. A Vietnam veteran could make a high school history class come alive. The grandmother around the corner has a postcard collection from the 1920s she could share.

This is an ongoing project because it will need to be updated fairly regularly. Start by deciding how large your directory readership will be: one school, one school district, several towns?

Next contact the appropriate administrator: the principal, the superintendent or superintendents. I can't imagine any administrator turning down such a valuable resource, but you need that person's cooperation.

Compile a list of people for possible inclusion. How? Send flyers home with students; make announcements at every meeting you attend, including at your church, business, or club. Talk up the

IF YOU'RE A PART-TIME WORKING PARENT

directory everywhere you go: your child's games and practices, parties, work, the park.

Once you have a list of at least fifty names, ask each person for his participation. By telephone is probably the easiest approach. Assure people that no one will ask for more than a few hours of their time and that they are free to handle a request according to their own schedule and convenience.

When you're ready to print the directory, give some thought to how it could be organized most effectively. For instance, by subject is probably more useful to a teacher than an alphabetical arrangement of strangers' names. For each listing you'll want to describe the person's area of interest or expertise, ways he could help a teacher, his "qualifications," a good time to reach him, and how to contact him. (See page 175 for a sample directory listing.)

87 ARRANGE INTERNSHIPS FOR STUDENTS IN THE COMMUNITY.

Internships can be wonderful learning experiences, especially for older children. Parents are often much better connected than teachers to the larger community and know where to find positions, including their own place of business. Internships can last for a few weeks, a few months, or the whole year. They can be paid or unpaid.

In Fort Worth, Texas, parents run a mini-internship program called "Vital Link" for middle schoolers. During the year, parents concentrate on finding jobs. Then in the summer, a student shadows an employer who explains job responsibilities and requirements so the student gains a more concrete understanding of work.

Contact your school's guidance counselor, principal, or youth employment coordinator to offer help. But don't rule out the person-to-person method, which works particularly well in a very small school system.

Sample Skills Directory Listing

SUBJECT: Social Studies, Geography, African-American Studies

SKILL OR SERVICE: Presentations on life in Kenya. Can provide videotapes, photographs, clothes, jewelry, and artifacts. Can prepare authentic Kenyan food. Can teach students a few words in the Kenyan national language.

BACKGROUND: I am an African-American who has been traveling to Kenya for the last ten years for business and pleasure.

CONTACT: Bruce Williams, (111) 222-3333 or e-mail: Bruce@prism.edu. Best times to call are after 7 p.m. on weekdays.

I know of one small computer game company, for example, that needed some temporary extra help. A parent who happened to work there and also lived nearby took the initiative to call the local high school, which had a student body of about 150. As she described what the company was looking for, she was transferred from a secretary to the vice principal to a guidance counselor to an English teacher. The English teacher immediately suggested a boy who was interested in computer programming, creativity, and trivia games. This young man wound up working after school for a few months and then during the summer at this company. Although he was hired to do routine tasks such as photocopying and fact-checking, by the end of his stint he had so impressed his supervisors, they let him write game questions. He had a ball, and the experience helped him get into his first-choice college.

88 BECOME A COMMUNITY COMMUNICATOR.

A community communicator does public relations for the school district. You can help stop rumors, spread facts, and act as a liaison. This works especially well if you are in a position that brings you into contact already with a large portion of the population on a regular basis (clergy, shopkeeper, police officer, hairdresser, doctor, gas station attendant). To see if your services could be of use in this way, call your district's main office. If they don't already have a program in place, suggest they call you on a regular basis to update you on any "hot" issues. You, in turn, can report back what you hear by way of comments and questions in the course of your day-to-day life.

89 LOBBY FOR AN ADVOCACY GROUP.

Advocacy groups usually focus on issues slightly outside of the curriculum or teaching. Some groups take a confrontational stance that I think weakens their position. I'd encourage you to keep your group supportive, rather than combative.

There are groups lobbying about the following and much more:

- Accessibility or accommodation for handicapped students.

- Tracking.

- Special programs.

- Tenure issues.

- Discrimination in the schools.

- Violence in the schools.

If there is a cause you would like to get involved in, find out if an existing advocacy group is working on that issue in your area by checking with the school board or the board of education. If not, you might want to start an advocacy or lobby group in your area. Begin by defining your mission, setting measurable goals, and gathering support in your community. Once you find a few like-minded people, organize a meeting to discuss the group's first actions, and distribute tasks. Good luck!

90 GET INVOLVED IN YOUR STATE LEGISLATURE.

There are several ways you can be involved with your state legislature. First, stay abreast of decisions made by state and local governing bodies and speak out when you have concerns or suggestions. Here are some ways to stay informed about what's happening in education:

- Subscribe to *Education Week,* a newspaper for pre-college educators (see page 205).

- Get on the mailing lists of the three organizations in your state that try to influence education legislation: the state school boards association, the state school administrators association, and the state teachers association.

- Stay in touch with local advocates and educators.

- Attend school board meetings.

After you are acquainted with the issues, there are a few ways to insert yourself in the process. One is by staying involved and vocal—going to meetings of the education committees on your state legislature and voicing your concerns. Another is to volunteer as an adviser to your state legislator. Who knows? You could end up as a legislator yourself someday. In the meantime, you can feel pride in the fact that you are getting—and staying—involved in education.

CHAPTER FIVE

CHALK IT UP

Dozens of organizations, Web sites, pamphlets, and materials for parents who want to go above and beyond.

Organizations

ACTIVE PARENTING
810 Franklin Ct., Suite B
Marietta, GA 30067
(800) 825-0060

Offers video-based/live discussion programs for educational professionals that address parenting issues.

ALLIANCE FOR PARENTAL INVOLVEMENT IN EDUCATION
P.O. Box 59
East Chatham, NY 12060
(518) 392-6900

Network that helps parents explore educational options, including public, private, and home schooling. In addition to a newsletter, ALLPIE publishes pamphlets on educational options and parents' rights. The organization sponsors workshops, retreats, and an annual family conference. Educational books and additional materials are available through ALLPIE's mail-order lending library and through its catalogue.

AMERICAN ASSOCIATION OF SCHOOL ADMINISTRATORS
1801 N. Moore St.
Arlington, VA 22209
(703) 528-0700

Founded in 1865, AASA is the professional organization for over 16,500 educational leaders across North America and worldwide. The organization focuses its efforts on improving the condition of children and youth; preparing schools and school systems for the next century; connecting schools and communities; and enhancing the quality and effectiveness of school leaders.

AMERICAN LIBRARY ASSOCIATION
50 East Huron St.
Chicago, IL 60611
(312) 944-6780

This 58,000–member organization is the oldest and largest library association in the world. It serves librarians, trustees, publishers, and other library supporters by representing public, school, academic, state, and special libraries serving government, commerce, armed services, hospitals, prisons, and other institutions.

ASPIRA ASSOCIATION
1444 I St. NW, Suite 800
Washington, DC 20005
(202) 835-3600

National nonprofit organization serving Puerto Rican and other Latino youth and their families, through leadership, education, and advocacy. Community service programs include mentoring, after-school activities, and APEX (Aspira Parents for Educational Excellence), a workshop designed to empower parents to help their children stay in and succeed in school. Publications available include training manuals, fact sheets on Hispanic health, education, and violence, and a newsletter.

ASSOCIATION FOR CHILDHOOD EDUCATION INTERNATIONAL
17904 Georgia Ave., Suite 215
Olney, MD 20832
(301) 570-2111

A national organization that works to promote the inherent rights, education, and well-being of all children in their homes, schools, and communities, ACEI seeks to raise the standard of awareness of those involved in the care and development of children.

BUSINESS PROFESSIONALS OF AMERICA
5454 Cleveland Ave.
Columbus, OH 43231
(614) 895-7277

Promotes leadership, citizenship, academic, and technical skills among middle and secondary school students, and provides networking opportunities for students and businesspeople.

CENTER FOR ADOLESCENT STUDIES
School of Education
Indiana University
Bloomington, IN 47405
(812) 856-8113

Works to meet the social and emotional growth and development needs of adolescents by providing support to adults working with them. Investigates current social issues and provides tools for teens to learn and practice new, healthy behaviors. Services include Drug Information Assessment and Decision Support, a computer-based decision aide to help schools select the drug prevention program most likely to meet their needs; Institute on Adolescents at Risk, a workshop that teaches skills to deal with teen risk taking and crisis intervention; and advice, strategies, and lesson plans for secondary teachers who want to enhance the social and emotional growth of their students.

CENTER FOR CIVIC EDUCATION
5146 Douglas Fir Road
Calabasas, CA 91302
(818) 591-9321

Funded by grants from the U.S. Department of Education, the Center for Civic Education is a nonprofit organization that promotes enlightened, competent, and responsible citizens. In addition to printed materials, the center sponsors student competitions of which parents serve as judges.

CENTER FOR THE STUDY OF PARENT INVOLVEMENT
12 Alta Rinda Rd.
Orinda, CA 94563
(510) 687-7362

Sponsors a national conference to help schools and communities encourage parental involvement in the educational process.

CENTER ON SCHOOL, FAMILY, AND COMMUNITY PARTNERSHIP
3003 N. Charles St., Suite 200
Baltimore, MD 21218
(410) 516-8800

Conducts and disseminates research, development, and policy analyses that produce new and useful knowledge and practices that help families, educators, and community members to work together to improve schools, strengthen families, and increase student success. Sponsors the National Network of Partnership–2000 Schools that guides schools, district and state leaders, and teams of educators, parents, and others to improve school, family, and community partnerships.

CHILDREN'S DEFENSE FUND
25 E St. NW
Washington, DC 20001
(202) 628-8787

Seeks through research, publications, public education, legislation, and other advocacy to provide a strong and effective voice for children. Sponsors Freedom Schools, a summer enrichment program for children that relies on parent participation. Also offers parent empowerment workshops that focus on conflict resolution, social action, and teaching parents how to be better advocates for their children.

COALITION OF ESSENTIAL SCHOOLS
Brown University
Box 1969
Providence, RI 02912
(401) 863-2847

A national network of schools and regional centers engaged in restructuring and redesigning schools to promote better student learning and achievement. Schools share a common set of ideas, known as the common principles, which guide their whole school reform efforts. The parent/school connection is an essential part of the program.

COMMUNITIES IN SCHOOLS
1199 North Fairfax St., Suite 300
Alexandria, VA 22314
(703) 519-8999

Communities in Schools is the nation's largest stay-in-school network, serving more than 300,000 young people through 121 local programs in 30 states. The mission of CIS is to champion the connection of needed community resources with schools to help young people successfully learn, stay in school, and prepare for life. By relocating community service providers to work as a personalized team serving alongside teachers, principals, volunteers, and mentors, CIS connects the community's existing resources with students and their families.

COUNCIL FOR EXCEPTIONAL CHILDREN
1920 Association Dr.
Reston, VA 20191
(703) 620-3660

The largest international professional organization dedicated to improving the educational outcome for both gifted and disabled students. Provides professional development opportunities and resources, printed materials, public policy advocacy, conventions, conferences, symposia, and standards for teachers, administrators students, parents, and related support service providers.

EDUCATION COMMISSION OF THE STATES
707 17th St., Suite 2700
Denver, CO 80202
(303) 299-3600

Nonprofit nationwide organization to help governors, state
legislators, state education leaders, and others develop policies to improve the quality of public education at all levels.

EDUCATION FUNDING RESEARCH COUNCIL
P.O. Box 22782
Tampa, FL 33622
(800) 876-0226

Provides publications that supply information on how to
gain federal funding and private grants for schools, nonprofit organizations, and government agencies.

EDUCATORS FOR SOCIAL RESPONSIBILITY
23 Garden St.
Cambridge, MA 02138
(617) 492-8820

A national nonprofit organization to help young people
develop the convictions and skills to build a safe, sustainable,
and just world. Promotes children's ethical and social development by advocating conflict resolution, violence prevention, intergroup relations, and character education. Provides
educators and parents with professional development support,
networking opportunities, and instructional materials.

ERIC CLEARINGHOUSE ON EDUCATIONAL MANAGEMENT
5207 University of Oregon
Eugene, OR 97403
(541) 346-5044; (800) 438-8841

The ERIC system is a nationwide educational information system to provide access to literature pertaining to every aspect of education. The Clearinghouse on Educational Management is one network of information processing and analysis centers. Pamphlets and articles on parent involvement in education are available.

FAMILY MATH
Lawrence Hall of Science
University of California
Berkeley, CA 94720
(510) 642-1823

A program that encourages parents and children to enjoy mathematics together. Books and an information packet are available that teach parents how to help their children with math.

FAMILY RESOURCE COALITION OF AMERICA
20 N. Wacker Dr., 11th floor
Chicago, IL 60606
(312) 338-0900

Publishes materials and offers technical assistance and consulting services for professionals who set up and maintain programs designed to strengthen and empower families and communities so that they can foster the optimal development of children, youth, and adult family members. FRCA also undertakes public education and advocacy campaigns and works to build networks among those in the family support field.

GRADS ORGANIZATION
P.O. Box 27437
San Diego, CA 92198
(888) 604-7237

A community-based, nonprofit organization formed as a preventative strategy in response to the alarming number of drug- and alcohol-related deaths on graduation night. GRADS has developed a network of concerned parents, school administrators, and other community volunteers who are committed to creating alcohol- and drug-free alternative activities for youth. Provides a manual, newsletter, and vendor directory, and functions as a resource center for Grad Night committees.

GRANDPARENT INFORMATION CENTER
601 E St. NW
Washington, DC 20049
(202) 434-2296

Program designed to help grandparents gain greater access to the public school system so that they can get information about their grandchildren's grades, report cards, and progress in school and make decisions about where their grandchildren attend school.

HOME AND SCHOOL INSTITUTE
1500 Massachusetts Ave. NW, Suite 42
Washington, DC 20005
(202) 466-3633

Sponsors the MegaSkills® Education Center, which helps families and educators build children's achievement in school and beyond through leader training seminars, teacher training, and school/family partnerships.

I HAVE A DREAM® FOUNDATION
330 Seventh Ave., 20th floor
New York, NY 10001
(212) 293-5480

"Adopts" children from public schools and public housing developments to participate in year-round programs of mentoring, tutoring, cultural exposure, and community service activities. Upon graduation, each child receives financial assistance for college or vocational education. Each IHAD project has an adult sponsor who maintains regular contact with the participants.

INFORMATION RESOURCE CENTER
U.S. Department of Education
600 Independence Ave. SW
Washington, DC 20202
(202) 401-2000

Provides brochures on family involvement as well as teaching materials for education professionals.

INSTITUTE FOR RESPONSIVE EDUCATION
Northeastern University
Boston, MA
(617) 373-2595

A national nonprofit organization committed to the belief that the best public schools are community institutions and community-building institutions, where everybody shares responsibility for educating all children. Operates the Responsive Schools Project, which coaches schools through a process of community engagement and school improvement. IRE assists the schools in creating partnership teams, conducting community-wide focus groups, identifying student competencies, setting priorities for improvement, planning for their improvement, and implementing and assessing their improvement plan.

INTERNATIONAL READING ASSOCIATION
800 Barksdale Rd.
Newark, DE 19711
(302) 731-1600

Provides programs and activities that develop young people's potential to become good citizens. Encourages student involvement in schools and communities.

JOBS FOR AMERICA'S GRADUATES
1729 King St., Suite 200
Alexandria, VA 22314
(703) 684-9479

Provides 42,000 at-risk and disadvantaged students in 550 high schools in 28 states with school-to-work transition and dropout prevention programs. Parents and students who volunteer to participate in the program are required to sign student/parent commitment forms.

LIONS YOUTH OUTREACH
Lions Clubs International
300 22nd St.
Oak Brook, IL 60523
(630) 571-5466, ext. 330

Encourages youth volunteerism as an alternative to violence, substance abuse, and gangs. Resources available are a teacher's guide, posters, and a video, *The Future Is Ours—So Now What?* Other programs sponsored are Lions-Quest Skills for Growing, Skills for Adolescence, and Skills for Actions, which stress substance abuse, violence prevention, and conflict resolution and are designed for presentation by schools. There is a strong parent component in all Lions Youth Outreach programs.

MEXICAN AMERICAN LEGAL DEFENSE AND
    EDUCATIONAL FUND
634 South Spring St., 11th floor
Los Angeles, CA 90014
(213) 629-2512

Offers a 12-week course for parents to empower them to be
better advocates for their children. Focuses on helping them
discover their basic rights as parents within the school system.

NATIONAL ACADEMY OF SCIENCES
2101 Constitution Ave.
Washington, DC 20418
(202) 334-2000

A private, independent, nonprofit organization that serves
as an official adviser to the federal government on science
and technology matters. Conducts studies and releases
reports on a variety of issues, including science education.

NATIONAL ALLIANCE OF BUSINESS
1201 New York Ave. NW, Suite 700
Washington, DC 20005
(202) 289-2925

A business-led nonprofit organization dedicated to building a
quality workforce that meets the needs of employers. Works
with the nation's business leaders as they take an active role in
building an internationally competitive workforce through
education reforms and enhanced job training.

NATIONAL ASSOCIATION FOR THE EDUCATION OF
  YOUNG CHILDREN
1509 16th St. NW
Washington, DC 20036
(800) 424-2460; (202) 232-8777

NAEYC is the nation's largest membership organization of early childhood professionals and others dedicated to improving the quality of services for young children and their families. A number of resources are available that address parent involvement in the education of young children.

NATIONAL ASSOCIATION OF PARTNERS IN EDUCATION
901 N. Pitt St., Suite 320
Alexandria, VA 22314
(703) 836-4880

The only national membership organization devoted solely to providing leadership in the formation and growth of effective partnerships that ensure success for all students. NAPE defines "partnership in education" as a collaborative effort between school or school district and one or more community organizations and businesses with the purpose of improving the academic and personal growth of America's youth. Joining in the partnership effort are parent organizations, businesses, universities, media, health care agencies, students, labor organizations, community clubs and organizations, foundations, and government.

NATIONAL BLACK CHILD DEVELOPMENT INSTITUTE
1023 15th St. NW, Suite 600
Washington, DC 20005
(202) 387-1281

An organization that works to improve and protect the quality of life for African-American children and their families through 40 chapters in communities throughout the United States. Some of these chapters offer programs that address parent involvement in their children's education.

NATIONAL CENTER FOR FAMILY LITERACY
325 West Main St., Suite 200
Louisville, KY 40202
(502) 584-1133

Organization dedicated to leadership through research, training, program development, and advocacy. All the programs stress the importance of parents and children learning together.

NATIONAL COALITION OF ADVOCATES FOR STUDENTS
100 Boylston St., Suite 737
Boston, MA 02116
(617) 357-8507

A national education advocacy organization with 22 member groups in 14 states that works to achieve equal access to a quality public education for children of color, economically disadvantaged students, recently immigrated children, and the disabled. Focusing on grades K–12, NCAS informs and mobilizes parents, children, educators, and communities to help resolve critical education issues. Sponsors Mobilization for Equity, a program that trains and supports parents to participate effectively in local school improvement efforts.

The National Asian Family School Partnership Project aims to expand the understanding of how public schools, Asian families, and Asian communities can build effective partnerships to support the school success of Asian students.

NATIONAL COUNCIL OF LA RAZA
1111 19th St. NW, Suite 1000
Washington, DC 20036
(202) 785-1670

Works to improve the opportunities of Hispanic Americans through a network of over 20,000 groups, coalitions, and individuals. Emphasis is on youth school-to-work apprenticeship programs and alternative methods for teaching Hispanic youth.

NATIONAL COUNCIL OF TEACHERS OF MATHEMATICS
1906 Association Dr.
Reston, VA 20191
(703) 620-9840

The mission of NCTM is to provide vision and leadership in improving the teaching and learning of mathematics so that every student is ensured an equitable standards-based mathematics education and every teacher of mathematics is ensured the opportunity to grow professionally.

NATIONAL DROPOUT PREVENTION CENTER
Clemson University
209 Martin St.
Clemson, SC 29634
(864) 656-2599

A nonprofit research center dedicated to addressing dropout prevention in grades K–12. Maintains a database with model programs that target parental involvement.

NATIONAL FAMILY PARTNERSHIP
9320 SW Barbur Blvd., Suite 340
Portland, OR 97219
(503) 244-5211

Promotes the formation of parent and youth groups to help prevent drug, tobacco, and alcohol abuse. Sponsors youth leadership training seminars that teach about the harmful effects of tobacco, alcohol, and other drugs and discourage their use. Participants are encouraged to return to their communities to use their newly-learned skills and to conduct drug education presentations in elementary schools and youth groups. Parent tool kits are available.

NATIONAL PARENT CENTER
1541 14th St. NW
Washington DC 20005
(202) 547-9286

Helps economically disadvantaged parents develop the
skills and abilities they need to make sound decisions with
the goal of improving the quality of their children's education. Sponsors training conferences and technical assistance
workshops. Printed materials are also available.

NATIONAL PTA
330 N. Wabash Ave., Suite 2100
Chicago, IL 60611
(312) 670-6782

Deals with a variety of education issues and develops current information, programs, and projects encouraging parents to participate in their children's education.

NATIONAL SCHOOL BOARDS ASSOCIATION
1680 Duke St.
Alexandria, VA 22314
(703) 838-6722

The mission of the NSBA, working with and through all
its federation members, is to foster excellence and equity in
public education through school board leadership.

ODYSSEY OF THE MIND
P.O. Box 547
Glassboro, NJ 08028
(609) 881-1603

Administered by OMK Association, Inc., a nonprofit organization, Odyssey of the Mind is a worldwide program that promotes creative team-based problem solving for kids from kindergarten through college. The program helps them learn divergent thinking and problem-solving skills while participating in a series of challenging and motivating activities, both inside and outside their regular classroom curriculum.

OPERATION OUTREACH–USA
10 Cochituate St.
Natick, MA 01760
(508) 650-4979

A national program that supports literacy, nonviolence, and character education for elementary school students. Each child who participates in the program receives two free books and a parent guide to facilitate parent participation.

PARENTS' RESOURCE INSTITUTE FOR DRUG EDUCATION
3610 Dekalb Technology Pkwy., Suite 105
Atlanta, GA 30340
(770) 458-9900

Provides a wide variety of drug prevention programs and services to parents, youth, community organizations, and educators in the United States and worldwide. Sponsors weekend retreats designed to instill the value of education, communication, and leadership.

PARTNERSHIP FOR FAMILY INVOLVEMENT IN EDUCATION
U.S. Department of Education
600 Independence Ave. SW
Washington, DC 20202
(800) 872-5327

A campaign organized by the federal government to promote children's learning through the development of family-school-community partnerships. Sponsors numerous programs such as Read*Write*Now! and America Goes Back to School. Provides extensive resources, including sample press releases, award certificates, and checklists, to family, school, employer, and religious groups.

PUBLIC EDUCATION INSTITUTE
Rutgers University
36 Street 1603
Piscataway, NJ 08854
(732) 463-1603

Sponsors monthly roundtable meetings to discuss public education issues. Participants include parents and school professionals (teachers, principals, and superintendents), leaders of education associations, legislators, foundation executives, and businesspeople.

PUBLIC EDUCATION NETWORK
601 13th St. NW, Suite 900N
Washington, DC 20005
(202) 628-7460

Assists local education foundations (LEFs) and other organizations in uniting and engaging their communities in building public schools that result in high achievement for every child. LEFs engage parents as key stakeholders by making information about school issues accessible, training parents in school-based management issues, linking families with technology, and providing resources for families.

SIMPLEX KNOWLEDGE COMPANY
P.O. Box 1260
White Plains, NY 10602
(914) 328-9400

A developer of *I See You!,* a video capture system for child care centers that enables parents to check in on their children using an encrypted password.

TEACH FOR AMERICA
20 Exchange Place, 8th floor
New York, NY 10005
(800) 832-1230

A national teacher corps of outstanding teacher graduates who commit two years to teach in disadvantaged areas throughout the United States.

UNITED CHILDREN'S FUND
700 13th St. NW, Suite 950
Washington, DC 20005
(202) 434-8917

A nonprofit general assistance fund for educational programs and services for children, UCF supports educational programs concerning drug abuse, health, and fitness; presents festival events for children and the general public; and produces and distributes public service announcements regarding family-child relationships.

WATCH ME
4851 Keller Springs Rd., Suite 221
Dallas, TX 75248
(972) 818-1828; (888) 592-8246

Produces a system for installation in schools and child care centers that allows parents to view images of their children while they're attending the programs.

WORK, ACHIEVEMENT, VALUES, AND EDUCATION
501 School St. SW, Suite 600
Washington, DC 20024
(202) 484-0103

WAVE provides educational opportunities, training, and motivation for young people facing barriers to success, at over 200 community, school, and workplace sites.

WORKING IN THE SCHOOLS
150 East Huron, Suite 900
Chicago, IL 60611
(312) 751-9487

A corps of over 200 men and women (most of whom are retired businesspersons and professionals) volunteer in inner-city Chicago elementary schools assisting teachers and working with the students.

Books

Beyond the Bake Sale: An Educator's Guide to Working with Parents, Anne Henderson, Carl Marburger, Theodora Ooms (Center for Law & Education, 1986).

Beyond the Classroom: Why School Reform Has Failed and What Parents Need to Do, Laurence Steinberg, Ph.D., B. Bradford Brown, Sanford M. Dornbusch (Touchstone Books, 1997).

Getting the Best Education for Your Child: A Parent's Checklist, James Keogh (Fawcett Books, 1997).

Parenting Our Schools: A Hands-On Guide to Education Reform, Jill Bloom (Little Brown & Company, 1992).

The Parents' Public School Handbook: How to Make the Most of Your Child's Education, from Kindergarten through Middle School, Kenneth Shore (Fireside, 1994).

Magazines and Pamphlets

Education Week, P.O. Box 2084, Marion, OH 43301, (800) 728-2790; $69.94/yr. (43 issues).

Helping Your Child Learn (series), Consumer Information Center, (719) 948-3334.

Learning Partners, Consumer Information Center, (719) 948-3334.

Moving America to the Head of the Class, Education Excellence Partnership, (202) 872-1260.

National Standards for Parent/Family Involvement Programs, National PTA, (312) 670-6782.

Strong Families, Strong Schools, U.S. Department of Education, (800) 872-5327.

Web Sites

CONNELLY-3-PUBLISHING GROUP
http://www.c3pg.com

Maintained by a publishing group that provides reading and learning materials for children ages three to ten, their parents, and early childhood education professionals. Also publishes the curriculum material for the Home Instruction Program for Preschool Youngsters (HIPPY), a home-based educational program for three-, four-, and five-year-olds. Provides links to other family/education–related sites.

CHOICES
http://www.choices.edfdn.org

An interactive, turnkey classroom seminar that teaches middle and high school students decision-making skills through creative participatory exercises.

THE EDUCATION SOURCE
http://www.edusource.com

Provides links to educational resources for parents, teachers, and home schoolers.

FAMILIES AND WORK INSTITUTE
http://www.familiesandwork.org

A national nonprofit research, strategic planning, and consulting organization that conducts policy and worksite research on the changing workforce and changing family/personal lives. Provides links to other sites devoted to education and family issues.

FAMILY EDUCATION NETWORK
http://www.familyeducation.com

A Web site devoted to parenting issues with links to schools, community centers, homework help, advice, and resources sites.

HAND IN HAND
http://www.handinhand.org

Hand in Hand, sponsored by the Mattel Foundation and coordinated by the Institute for Educational Leadership, shares information about programs that expect, value, and nurture a family and community role in children's learning. This site has links to other Web resources that encourage parent participation in the educational process.

HANDSNET
http://www.handsnet.org.

A national, nonprofit organization that promotes information sharing, cross-sector collaboration, and advocacy among individuals and organizations working on a broad range of public interest issues, including parent involvement in education. The site maintains forums and links to recent headlines that concern parenting and to the Youth Development Forum, an online clearinghouse for education resources.

INSTITUTE FOR EDUCATIONAL LEADERSHIP
http://www.iel.org

Seeks to strengthen educational opportunities for children and youth by connecting leaders from different ethnic and racial sectors and by reconnecting the public with educational institutions. Maintains links to related sites.

NATIONAL ALLIANCE FOR BUSINESS
http://www.nab.com

Maintains links to resources devoted to improving schools.

PARENT POWER
http://www.parentpower.org

A nonprofit organization based in Indiana that sponsors projects to promote parent involvement in the education of K–12 students. The Web site maintains links to parent resources.

PARENTS AS TEACHERS
http://www.patnc.org

An organization that helps parents acquire the skills to help make the most of their children's early-learning years. The program teaches child development; suggests activities that encourage language development, intellectual growth; social and motor skills; and strengthens the parent-child relationship.

GLOSSARY

Italicized words within definitions are also in this glossary.

ability grouping: A common instructional practice of clustering students according to their academic skills in classrooms. Ability grouping allows a teacher to provide the same level of instruction to the entire group. See *tracking* and page 45.

accreditation: The process by which an organization, usually the National Council for the Accreditation of Teacher Education, sanctions teacher-education programs. The council gives certain programs—about 500 of the some 1,300 that prepare teachers—its seal of approval for quality. States also approve teacher-education programs, by means of issuing teaching licenses to their graduates.

achievement test: A test designed to measure what a student has learned in a certain subject.

Advanced Placement: A series of courses administered by the College Board that high school students can take to earn college credit. Students must master a generally higher level of coursework and pass an accompanying test.

alternative assessment: Any form of measuring what students know and are able to do other than traditional standardized tests. Alternative forms of assessment include *portfolios, performance-based assessments,* and other means of testing students.

annual review: A yearly review mandated by federal law that evaluates a student's *special education* program.

aptitude test: A test, designed to evaluate a student's capacity for learning, which is often used to predict future performance.

at risk: Describes a student with socioeconomic challenges, such as poverty or teen pregnancy, which may place them at a disadvantage in achieving academic, social, or career goals. Such students are deemed "at risk" of failing, dropping out, or "falling through the cracks" at school.

attention-deficit disorder (ADD): A disorder characterized by the inability to concentrate and, in some cases, impulsiveness and hyperactivity. Between 3 and 10 percent of the nation's school-age children are thought to have the disorder. Some children qualify for special-education services on the basis of having this disorder. The children who are hyperactive are often labeled ADHD, for attention-deficit/hyperactivity disorder.

basal readers: Elementary schoolbooks that incorporate simple stories and practice exercises to reinforce what students are learning.

basic skills: The traditional building blocks of a *curriculum* that are most commonly associated with explicit instruction in early elementary language arts and mathematics. Basic skills, historically taught in isolation, include teaching the letters of the alphabet, how to sound out words, spelling, grammar, counting, adding, subtracting, and multiplying.

bilingual education: An educational program designed for students whose first language is not English. Material is presented in two languages while the student gradually receives more English language instruction.

Buckley amendment: A federal law that controls who has access to a child's school records. Parents are given access to the records, and are allowed to challenge the contents, while access by other parties is restricted. Otherwise known as the Family Educational Rights and Privacy Act.

Carnegie Unit: A credit representing the completion of a core of high school courses. Developed in the early 1900s to set norms for curriculum and course time in public schools across the country, these are named after the Carnegie Foundation for the Advancement of Teaching, which first suggested the practice.

character education: Deliberate instruction in basic virtues or morals, as opposed to weaving these values into every lesson. A national movement is under way to include character education in school curricula as one means of alleviating the current deficit in school children's values by strengthening their moral fiber.

charter schools: Schools run independently of the traditional public school system but receiving public funding, run by groups such as teachers, parents, or foundations. Charter schools are free of many district regulations and are often tailored to community needs.

College Board (or College Entrance Examination Board): A nonprofit organization that assists students in moving from secondary education into higher education. The College Board is composed of colleges, universities, and other agencies and associations that provide services to secondary and post-secondary students. Programs administered by the College Board include the *Scholastic Assessment Test* and the *Advanced Placement* program, among others.

cooperative learning: A method of instruction that encourages students to work in small groups to learn material, then present the material to other small groups. In doing so, they take responsibility for their own learning as well as that of their classmates.

critical thinking: The mental process of acquiring information, then evaluating it to reach a logical conclusion or answer. Increasingly, educators believe that schools should focus more on critical thinking than on memorization of facts.

cumulative record: The collected records on a particular student. These might include report cards, standardized test results, correspondence, awards, or disciplinary action.

curriculum: The subject matter that teachers and students cover in class.

decentralization: In education, the term is most frequently used to describe the transfer of school policy-making authority from the federal to the state level, or the transfer of decision-making authority from the state level to districts or schools.

distance learning: The use of telecommunications technologies, including satellites, telephones, and cable-television systems, to broadcast instruction from one central site to one or more remote locations. Typically, a television image of a teacher is broadcast to students in remote locations. This may also be done using interactive videoconferencing. Rural districts frequently use distance learning so one teacher can teach students in more than one school at once.

dyslexia: A reading impairment, thought to be a genetic condition, which affects up to 10 percent of the nation's schoolchildren. One trait of dyslexia might be transposing letters. Children born to parents with dyslexia may be eight times as likely to have the condition.

emotional and behavioral disorders: Also called EBDs, disorders characterized by consistently aggressive, impulsive, or withdrawn behavior, including schizophrenia. Each state classifies these conditions differently. Clinicians generally consider behavior to be an EBD if it impairs personal, social, academic, and vocational skills.

enrichment: Enrichment programs—originally designed primarily for gifted students, but now widely used with at-risk children as well—are intended to supplement the regular academic curriculum for students who might otherwise be bored with their classwork. For the gifted, they are an alternative to acceleration, so that even the brightest students can remain in class with children their own age and maturity, yet be adequately challenged. Sometimes run as pull-out programs, enrichment programs are also an alternative to creating entirely separate gifted classrooms. Enrichment is intended to add value to the curriculum, often in a fun way, through such activities as special projects, guest speakers, concerts, and museum visits. Many educators have found that what was originally considered enrichment is actually worth incorporating into the regular curriculum.

gender bias: Conscious or unconscious differential treatment—in a textbook or by a teacher or employer—of females and males based on their sex.

gifted students: Pupils who are considered to have the capacity to achieve beyond the norm—either because of their IQ scores, their demonstrated ability in the classroom, or both. Once limited to academic skills, the definition of giftedness in many schools is expanding to include children with a wide variety of talents.

Goals 2000: A federal program that provides grants to states and school districts in exchange for the establishment of challenging academic content standards and accompanying assessments. It codifies the six national education goals that emerged from the 1989 education summit of President Bush and the nation's governors. Introduced by the Clinton administration and adopted by Congress in 1993, Goals 2000 has now expanded to eight national education goals.

grade-level equivalent: A test score that refers to the grade level at which a student performs compared to the student's real grade level. Allows evaluation of the student that extends beyond the current curriculum. A 3.5 grade-level equivalent on a standardized test, for example, means a student, no matter how old, is performing like an average child in the fifth month of third grade.

home schooling: The practice of parents teaching their children at home rather than sending them to public school. According to the U.S. Department of Education, an estimated 500,000 students—one percent of the nation's school-age population—are now home schooled.

inclusion: The practice of educating children with disabilities alongside their non-disabled peers, often in a regular classroom in their neighborhood school. The *Individuals with Disabilities Education Act* requires that disabled children be educated in the "least restrictive environment" possible. Also called full inclusion. See *special education*.

independent school: A private or nonpublic school that is not part of a state school system. An independent school is governed by a board of trustees instead of by the state board of education. It is funded by tuition and private donations and grants. The school must hold a nonprofit status and be accredited by an approved state or regional association. It must be nondiscriminatory, and can be either religious or nonreligious.

individualized education program (IEP): A written plan that describes the educational program for an educationally disabled student.

Individuals with Disabilities Education Act (IDEA): A landmark 1975 federal law, originally known as the Education for All Handicapped Children Act. In exchange for federal money, schools must guarantee that all children with disabilities receive a "free, appropriate public education." Different portions of the law cover children from birth to age 21. The law has been amended several times but originally addressed children with disabilities who were kept out of the public schools and taught either at home or in institutions.

invented spelling: The process of spelling words as they sound, which is practiced by young children who are learning to read and write.

Iowa Tests of Basic Skills: General achievement tests for grades three through eight. Along with others, such as the Comprehensive Tests of Basic Skills and the Stanford Achievement Test Series, they are designed to measure how well a student has learned the basic knowledge and skills that are taught in elementary and middle schools, in such areas as reading and mathematics.

IQ: Acronym for intelligence quotient, which is a person's purported mental capacity. IQ tests have become increasingly controversial because critics claim they measure only a narrow band of intellectual strengths, primarily academic ability. Others claim the tests are biased against members of some minority groups.

Kentucky Education Reform Act: The nation's most sweeping state school-reform law. Passed by the Kentucky

General Assembly in 1990, it enacted new curriculum, governance, finance, and technology initiatives. The law grew out of a 1989 state supreme court decision.

learning disabilities: Encompasses a wide variety of learning difficulties; the criteria for the label varies from state to state. In general, a learning disability describes a discrepancy between a child's intelligence and academic achievement. Some children have learning disabilities only in specific areas, such as reading or math.

Limited-English-proficient students: Students who speak a language other than English. They are either immigrants or children born in the United States. Each state has a different way of ascertaining whether a child is limited-English-proficient. Usually such students receive bilingual-education or English-as-a-second-language services.

magnet school: A school that places special emphasis on academic achievement or on a particular field such as science or art, designed to attract students from elsewhere in the school district.

mainstream: To include an educationally disabled student in regular classes for those subjects in which the student is capable of doing the required work without special education support.

master teachers: Experienced teachers who work with newer teachers or with teachers who are having trouble in the classroom to help them become more effective.

merit pay: Any of a number of plans to pay teachers on the basis of their demonstrated competence in teaching. The pay plans are controversial because it is difficult to objectively identify good teaching, and many argue that such plans would be little more than popularity contests.

multicultural education: An educational philosophy and curriculum that looks beyond curricula from the white Western European tradition. Some multicultural education models highlight subjects from diverse cultural, ethnic, racial, and gender perspectives. Others represent an immersion in one culture, ethnicity, or race.

multimedia: Software that combines text, sound, video, animation, and graphics into a single presentation. The multimedia format is frequently used in "edutainment" software. An example of multimedia would be an electronic encyclopedia in CD-ROM format.

norm group: A designated standard of average performance of students of a given age, background, or geographic location.

norm-referenced test: A test comparing a student's performance with other students in the same grade or of the same age, based on a numerical score.

outcomes-based education: An education theory that guides curriculum by setting goals for students to accomplish. Outcomes-based education focuses more on these goals, or outcomes, than on inputs, or subject units. This theory has drawn intense criticism from parent groups who fear that, by focusing on outcomes, schools are deciding on goals for students which may conflict with the goals of the students and parents.

parochial school: A school that is church-related, most commonly to the Roman Catholic Church but also to other denominations. Hebrew day schools can also be termed parochial.

pay equity: Paying teachers based on a single-salary schedule that pays men and women and elementary and secondary teachers the same. Teachers are paid according to how many years they have been teaching and how many educational credits or degrees they have accumulated.

percentile rank: A test score that shows how well a student performed compared with other students in the norm group of the same grade or age group.

performance-based assessment: Requires students to perform hands-on tasks, such as writing an essay or conducting a science experiment. Such assessments are becoming increasingly common as alternatives to multiple-choice, machine-scored tests. Also known as authentic assessment.

phonics: An instructional strategy used to teach letter-sound relationships to beginning readers by having them sound out words.

portfolio: A systematic and organized collection of a student's work throughout a course or class year. It measures the student's knowledge and skills and often includes some form of self-reflection by the student.

privatization: Transfer of the management of public schools to private or for-profit education organizations. Privatization emphasizes typical business-oriented concepts such as customer satisfaction and managerial autonomy in running schools.

reform network: An association of educators, schools, or districts joined together to provide mutual support as they work on common plans for improving education. Popular reform networks include Theodore Sizer's Coalition of Essential Schools and James Comer's School Development Program.

remedial education: Instruction that seeks to bring students deficient in basic skills up to standard levels in essential subjects such as writing, reading, and math.

report cards: The periodic evaluations of a student's academic progress, usually sent home to parents. Report cards comparing a schools' performance require districts to inform the public about how well each school is doing by means of student test scores and other measures.

Scholastic Assessment Test (SAT): The SAT is a standardized test, usually taken by college-bound students. The SAT I: Reasoning Test measures verbal and mathematical reasoning ability. It is designed to predict who will do well in college. The SAT II: Subject Test, formerly known as Achievement Tests, measures current ability and knowledge in specific high school subject areas such as English and biology.

school-based management: The shift of decision-making authority from school districts to individual schools. Such systems vary, but they usually give control of a school's operation to a school council composed of parents, teachers, and local administrators. See *site-based management*.

school-community services: Activities offered on or near school sites to benefit families and other neighborhood residents. Such activities include child care, adult education, recreation, counseling, health screening, mentoring, tutoring, conflict resolution, parent education, job training, cultural and arts programs, or drop-in centers for teenagers.

school reform: A generic term encompassing all kinds of efforts that are taking place to improve schools. Reform efforts focus on all aspects of schooling, from how schools are governed to what curriculum is taught in the classroom.

school-to-work transition: Any of a host of programs from on-the-job training to apprenticeships to cooperative agreements between high schools and community colleges designed to prepare students not bound for college to enter the job market.

service learning: Programs that incorporate citizenship values into education by requiring students to perform community service. In some districts, community service is a mandatory requirement for graduation.

site-based management: The shift of decision-making authority from centralized bureaucracies to local individual establishments. Such proposals vary, but they usually give control of an organization's operation to local administrators. See *school-based management*.

special education: Programs designed to serve children with mental and physical disabilities. Such children are entitled to individualized education plans that spell out the services needed to reach their educational goals, ranging from speech therapy to math tutoring. Traditionally, special education has taken place in separate classrooms. Increasingly, the services may also be offered in regular schools and classrooms.

standards: Subject-matter benchmarks to measure students' academic achievement. Curriculum standards drive what students learn in the classroom. Most agree that public schools' academic standards need to be raised. However, there is national debate over how to implement such standards—how prescriptive they should be, and whether they should be national or local, voluntary or mandated.

stanine: One of the nine categories of performance into which standardized test scores are divided, with one the lowest and nine the highest. The average falls in the four to six range. The stanine score is a more accurate measure of a child's overall performance. While a student's percentile may change, his or her stanine score will generally remain the same, providing a more accurate view of the child's level of performance compared to that of his or her peers.

teacher certification: A process through which teachers become recognized by the state as expert teachers, implying that a teacher has mastered the complex art of teaching. This is distinguished from a licensed teacher, one who practices teaching but is not considered an expert.

teacher licensure: The process by which teachers receive state permission to teach. States typically have such minimum requirements as the completion of certain coursework and experience as a student teacher. Some states, faced with shortages of teachers in particular areas, grant teachers emergency licenses and allow them to take required courses while they are full-time teachers.

Title I: The nation's largest federal education program. Created in 1965 during the War on Poverty, Title I of the Elementary and Secondary Education Act serves remedial education programs to poor and disadvantaged children in nearly every school district in the country. Amendments to the law in 1994 were designed to tie the program to schoolwide and districtwide reforms based on challenging academic standards.

Title IX: Bars gender discrimination in education facilities that receive federal funds. The full name of the law is Title IX of the Education Amendments of 1972. Title IX cases, which have typically been filed at the college level, have increasingly been filed against K–12 schools for sex equity in extracurricular sports.

Title VII: A federal program to help limited-English-proficient students. The full title of this program, created in 1984, is Title VII of the Elementary and Secondary Education Act. Funding goes to alternative approaches to bilingual education, such as English immersion programs, as well as traditional instruction in a student's native language.

tracking: The practice of placing students with the same level of ability in the same class, allowing the teacher to adjust the pace of instruction according to the students' needs. For more information on tracking, see page 45. Also called *ability grouping*.

vocational education: Instruction that prepares a student for employment immediately after the completion of high school. Although often thought of in terms of shop or carpentry courses, such programs frequently also include a strong academic component and teach such skills as computer-aided design.

vouchers: A document or chit, usually issued by the state, that can be used by parents to pay tuition at an out-of-district public school, a private school, or a religious school. The term is also used more broadly to describe school-choice proposals in which states would help pay tuition for children attending private or religious schools.

whole language: A philosophy and instructional strategy that emphasizes reading for meaning and in context. Although teachers may give phonics lessons to individual students as needed, the emphasis is on teaching students to use language as a whole, rather than as skills broken down into parts. Students learn language by using it as they study various subjects.

year-round education: A modified school calendar that offers short breaks throughout the year, rather than the traditional long summer vacation. The calendars vary as do the reasons for switching to a year-round schedule. Some schools stagger the schedules to relieve crowding. Others think during a three-month summer break students forget much of the material covered in the previous year.

APPENDIX

A Sample Kindergarten Curriculum

Kindergarten classes are heterogeneous in nature. In addition to the subject areas listed below, a primary focus of the kindergarten program is to orient the children to school procedures and to provide many experiences that promote social and emotional growth.

LANGUAGE ARTS

The "Language Arts" program helps children learn all modes of communication: experiencing, listening, speaking, observing, illustrating. Children learn best when surrounded by an environment rich in multisensory experiences. Learning centers are organized around topics and themes that lend themselves to extensions, integrating all of the disciplines: art, music, math, science, etc.

Through shared literature experiences, children are able to participate in creative follow-up activities. They are encouraged to express their ideas in picture and written form often generating original books, collaborative posters, and murals as a prelude to reading. Through dramatizations, tapes, music, and body movement they develop their skills in a holistic context.

While children are developing an appreciation for literature, opportunity is also provided for them to begin experiencing the sounds and symbols of beginning phonics.

MATH

"Math Their Way," a program with a wide variety of manipulative materials, is used. This is an activity-centered program based on developing understanding and insight into the patterns of mathematics through the use of concrete materials.

The units of instruction include:

- Free exploration
- Patterning
- Sorting and classifying
- Counting
- Comparing graphing
- Number

SCIENCE

The science program is a hands-on curriculum with life science and physical science modules. Children learn to observe, predict, hypothesize, classify, experiment, and organize data. The units of instruction include:

- Farm and wild animals
- Color and light
- Magnets
- Senses
- Weather and seasons
- Water and rain
- Sinking and floating

- Growing seeds
- Hatching chicks

SOCIAL STUDIES

In social studies, we deal with aspects of our culture that are close to the children's experiences, such as holidays and current events. Units are designed to help youngsters know who and what they are, thus developing a sense of identity. "All About Me" books created by the children are a cumulative outgrowth of the entire year. Through interviews, graphs, charts, presentations, and international week, children are able to understand change, responsibility, service to others, and citizenship.

ART

Art is provided by the art specialist. In addition, art is integrated into the curriculum with emphasis on process, individuality, skills, and creativity. Through various media, children are encouraged to express themselves. Projects relate to classroom subject matter, seasons, holidays, and the community. Media include crayon, chalk, paint, magic marker, collage materials, clay, tissue paper, finger paint, yarn, acrylic, and elements of nature. Through these experiences children develop a sense of self and a more accurate perspective of their place within the environment.

A Sample Fourth Grade Curriculum

MATH

1. Writing and reading numerals to one million
2. Decimal point—adding and subtracting decimals
3. Ordinal numbers
4. Patterning
5. Place value to one million
6. Zero as a placeholder
7. Rounding to nearest thousand
8. Roman numerals
9. Subtraction with regrouping
10. Addition
11. Multiplication facts to 100. Division facts to 100. Inverse operations.
12. 2 x 2 digit multiplication
13. 3 x 2 digit division
14. Story problems
15. Number sentences with missing factors
16. Estimating sums
17. Factoring numbers
18. Fractions—add, subtract, reduce to lowest terms with like denominator

19. Graphs (line, bar, and circle)

20. Averaging

21. Perimeter

22. Metric—length, mass, capacity to milli, metric symbols

23. Checking addition, subtraction, multiplication, and division

24. Division—up to three-digit divisors

LANGUAGE

1. Definition, classification, and function of nouns, verbs, pronouns, and adjectives

2. Identify subject and predicate (simple and complete)

3. Four kinds of sentences and end marks

4. Contractions, prefixes, suffixes, homonyms, and antonyms

5. Recognition of topic sentence

6. Friendly letters, business letters

7. Capitalization for geographical names, businesses, months, days, books, proper nouns

8. Punctuation—question marks, commas, apostrophes

9. Handwriting

10. Speaking skills—inflection, pronunciation, oral reports

11. Listening skills—patience, interest

12. Paragraph building
13. Can compose a short anecdote
14. Creative writing—beginning, middle, end
15. Dictionary skills—syllabication, pronunciation, multiple meanings
16. Spelling

READING

1. Main idea in a series of paragraphs
2. Details and their relationship to main idea
3. Figurative language, idioms, metaphors, similes, inferences, cause/effect
4. Phonetic and structural analysis—phonetic irregularities and decoding 3-, 4-, 5-syllable words
5. Parts of a book
6. Skimming, sequencing, recognizing key words
7. Outlining—topic and subtopic
8. Following directions
9. Readings charts, graphs, and maps
10. Vocabulary development and mastery
11. Reading comprehension

SCIENCE

1. Electricity and magnets
2. Minerals and rocks

3. Matter and energy

4. Air, light (eye), sound (ear)

5. Living things and adaptations and behavior

6. The oceans

SOCIAL STUDIES

1. Discovery, exploration, settlement of New World

2. Indians of the Northeast

3. New York State and local history

4. Biographical, chronological overview of famous Americans

5. Map studies and general geographic concepts and map legend and key

6. Current events

Sample Grad Night Letter #2 to Parents

Lincoln High School '97 Grad Night
The Ultimate Graduation Party

To keep our graduates safe this year, Lincoln High School is offering a Grad Night party for all graduates in the Lincoln District and we are asking for your support. A committee of parents and staff have been working very hard since October planning and constructing in order to transform the McCandless School into an amusement park–type atmosphere. We want to provide our students with an unforgettable evening of fun, excitement, exhilaration, and quiet moments. It will be a time for renewing old friendships and a time for goodbyes. This party will be unlike anything your child has experienced before. Grads can enjoy activities such as casino games, carnival games, karaoke, DJ, videos, magicians, beach volleyball, and much, much more. We will also be providing unlimited food and beverages for the evening as well as prizes (stereos, TVs, radios, cameras, cash, etc.), which all add to the excitement of the event.

The all-night grad party will take place at McCandless School, on graduation night, June 5, 1997, 10 p.m. until 5 a.m. The party is open to those students who will graduate in June from one of the schools in the Lincoln District. The gates will close at 11 p.m. This will give the students time to go home after graduation, celebrate for a short time with their families, change into comfortable clothes, and be ready for Grad Night! Once students have entered the party area, they may leave only if parents or guardians have been notified by phone. If your student has purchased a ticket for Grad Night and does not arrive by 11 p.m., someone from the Grad Night Committee will be calling you as soon as possible.

As part of the experience we are planning a display of baby pictures and home videos. If you have a baby picture of your senior and/or home videos (which can include from babyhood to the present), we would appreciate your sharing them with us. Pictures and videos will be returned. Please put your name and phone number on each and drop them off in the Student Service Center at Lincoln High to either Suzanne Krenecki or Carol Mitchell.

The cost of a ticket for the event is $25 until April 30th, $30 until May 31st, and $35 until the day before graduation. Ticket sales are held every Friday at lunch time in front of the school. There will be a special drawing the week before graduation for the first 100 students who purchase their ticket. The use of a limousine for the winner on graduation night will be the prize.

If you have any questions about Grad Night, please contact Sandy DeGuire.

Sample Publicity Release/Letter

Today Feature Editor
The Record
Stockton, CA 95202

Dear Editor,

Lincoln High School GRAD NIGHT Committee
is planning a special celebration for the senior
class of '97. We would like to invite you to
become a participant and contributor in this
wonderful gift for the youth of our community.

By offering an alternative to traditional reckless
"partying", grads can attend an all night celebration produced entirely by parents and supported
by the community. A safe environment replaces
the potential dangers of being on the streets,
drunk driving and violence. With your help it is
our hope that this GRAD NIGHT will be a night
every Lincoln High graduate will remember.

We would appreciate the opportunity to be
featured in the Today section of The Record. A
feature article would surely add to the importance and excitement of this event. We have been
overwhelmed by the participation of the Stockton
business community in supporting Lincoln's first
ever GRAD NIGHT, and the concern the community has for keeping our youth safe. We wish to
thank you in advance for your consideration.

Publishing Center Manuscript/Cover Instruction Form

Here are the instructions the parent volunteers refer to throughout the process:

Before the student arrives for his/her appointment:

- Pull a manuscript instruction form, library display sheet, and baggie for each student. (For examples of the manuscript/cover instruction form and the library display sheet, see pages 84–85.)

Once student arrives:

- Have student choose book cover and lining paper (sulfite).
- Fill out manuscript instruction form with child. Remember to fill out dedication and about the author sections if they are not included in the student's rough draft.
- Ask the student if he/she would like to display the finished book in the library, and if so, complete the library display sheet.

1. Check spelling.
2. Insert page breaks (pages must end with a complete sentence).
3. Make sure student is happy with placement of illustrations and text (especially if text is rearranged for page breaks and does not line up with illustrations).

- Send student back to classroom.

Once student has gone back to classroom:

Make a mock copy of the book for the typists:

1. Refer to chart on table which indicates how many sheets of paper will be needed per pages of text, and pull that number.

2. Fold rough draft sheets in half, lengthwise.

3. Write lightly in pencil, on outside corner of each page:
   Title, dedication
   Number pages 1, 2, 3...
   Disclaimer (second to last page)
   About the author (last page)

Place the following in a baggie, and put in TO BE TYPED bin:

1. Manuscript/instruction form

2. Library display sheet, if applicable

3. Student's manuscript

4. Book cover

5. Lining paper

6. Mock rough draft copy for typist

Making book covers:

1. Plug in and turn on iron—no water, permanent-press setting.

2. Pull fabric, dry-mount paper, and two cardboard sheets.

3. Iron fabric to get out any wrinkles.

4. Place fabric right side down on table, cover with dry-mount paper.

5. Center cardboard over fabric/dry mount and put spine guard in center.

6. Press cardboard, being careful not to touch dry-mount paper.

7. Remove spine guard, and turn over to iron right side of fabric.

8. Turn back over, and fold and press corners.

9. Fold over and press sides.

10. Close the book, and iron outside on both sides.

11. Weigh down for fifteen minutes.

Binding books

1. Take baggie containing typed book from TO BE BOUND bin.

2. Erase pencil markings.

3. Fold lining paper.

4. Place typed sheets inside lining paper.

5. Flatten book and line up with a ruler.

6. Use chart to mark book for sewing and make holes.

Seasonal Suggestions

Any parent of a school-aged child is in tune with the natural rhythm of the academic year. So I've included this month-by-month section for you to check for ways to get involved that are appropriate at various times of the school year. You can also jot notes relating to your involvement, or perhaps even use these pages to set parental involvement goals for yourself.

SEPTEMBER

Write important dates in the calendar.

(**7** Make a family calendar.)

OCTOBER

Call the superintendent about math program.

(22 Make a point of calling your school district

superintendent.)

NOVEMBER

Don't forget election day!

(71 Form an election committee.)

DECEMBER

Bring in the Ukrainian Christmas ornaments.

(**42** Share a collection or a custom.)

JANUARY

Make a detective costume for reading Sherlock Holmes.

(**62** Be a mystery reader.)

FEBRUARY

Write list of questions for conference.

(**39** Prepare ahead for a parent-teacher conference.)

MARCH

Meet with kids in guidance office to go over resumes.

(**65** Be a career consultant.)

APRIL

Talk to Ms. McNamara about next year's teacher.

(**15** Write a letter to your child's school principal

in the spring.)

MAY

Check to make sure cumulative file is complete before

Jay starts middle school.

(**20** Review your child's school records.)

JUNE

Chaperone senior dance!

(**58** Hold a safe graduation night.)

SUMMER

Start research in preparation for fall planning meeting.

(**81** Start a local education foundation.)

INDEX